The Edna Lewis Cookbook

Books by
Edna Lewis

The Edna Lewis Cookbook, 1972
(with Evangeline Peterson)

The Taste of Country Cooking, 1976

In Pursuit of Flavor, 1988
(with Mary Goodbody)

The Gift of Southern Cooking, 2003
(with Scott Peacock)

The
Edna Lewis
Cookbook

Edna Lewis &
Evangeline Peterson

Introduction by
Hunter Lewis

AXIOS

Axios Press
PO Box 457
Edinburg, VA 22824
888.542.9467   info@axiosinstitute.org

Library of Congress Cataloging-in-Publication Data

Names: Lewis, Edna author. | Peterson, Evangeline author.
Title: The Edna Lewis cookbook / Edna Lewis & Evangeline Peterson.
Description: Edinburg, VA : AXIOS, [2016] | Includes an index.
Identifiers: LCCN 2016023287 | ISBN 9781604191066 (pbk.)
Subjects: LCSH: Cooking. | Menus. | LCGFT: Cookbooks.
Classification: LCC TX714 .L49 2016 | DDC 641.5--dc23 LC record available at https://lccn.loc.gov/2016023287

For

NINA, EDWARD, AND RALPH

Contents

Outdoor Summer Menus   45

Autumn & Winter Dinner Menus   55

Luncheon Menus   91

Buffet Dinners   107

Outdoor Summer Buffet   121

Photo Credits

Introduction

Edna Lewis (1916–2006)

The principal author of this cookbook was a black woman who rose from humble origins and almost singlehandedly revived fine Southern cooking. Thanks to her, this style of food is not only increasingly popular in America, but also admired around the world. Those who love this sometimes simple but often complicated and sophisticated food and regard it as one of the world's great cuisines owe a lot to the woman who has been referred to as the "*Grande Dame* of Southern cooking" and "the South's answer to Julia Child."

The famous American chef James Beard said, "Edna Lewis makes me want to go right into the kitchen and start cooking." That is how many people feel about her. The US government honored her achievement with a commemorative postal stamp acknowledging her place among the greatest American chefs. The stamp is a head shot, so you don't see her tall, lithe body, often clothed in African fabrics, or her dignified way of moving and talking. "You couldn't walk down the street without people stopping [her]: 'You're so beautiful I want to paint you, photograph you,'" reports Scott Peacock, former executive chef of Watershed Restaurant in Decatur, Georgia, a famous Southern chef himself, and co-author of her last book.

Lewis also had a gift for living and for friendship. She counted friends among the poorest and the richest of Americans. She listened carefully and thoughtfully to everyone's concerns and offered advice that was always grounded in common sense but that nevertheless came straight from the heart. No wonder so many people loved her. And she knew how to live. Everything she touched came alive with inspiration and pleasure, even simple tasks such as selecting food or preparing a meal.

Edna Lewis was born on April 13, 1916, in Freetown, Virginia, a small town established and named by three former slaves, including her grandfather Chester Lewis. She was one of eight children. The families in Freetown were largely self-sufficient, foraging or raising their own food and meat, with a few purchases from a nearby general store. Water was pumped by hand from the ground and heat in the winter was by wood fire or old Franklin Stove.

Of life in Freetown, Lewis said: "If someone borrowed one cup of sugar, they would return two. If someone fell ill, the neighbors would go in and milk the cows, feed the chickens, clean the house, cook the food and come and sit with whoever was sick. I guess rural life conditioned people to cooperate with their neighbors."

What the family ate changed with the seasons. Lewis learned to cook (on a wood stove) by watching and imitating the other women of the family. Where tools were lacking, the cooks improvised. For example, they could not afford measuring spoons, so measured homemade baking powder on coins.

After leaving Freetown at age 16 to earn money for the family, Lewis moved to Washington, DC and then to New York. Jobs included ironing (she did not really know how to iron and lost that job within hours), domestic work, and seamstress. After making dresses for celebrities such as Marilyn Monroe, she became the window "dresser" at Bonwit Teller, a fashionable department store, an important and well paid job, but in 1948 left to become chef and partner at Café Nicholson, a new restaurant owned by a friend, a wealthy and well connected New York Bohemian named John Nicholson. Customers included Paul Robeson, Tennessee Williams, Gore Vidal, Truman Capote, William Faulkner, Richard Avedon, Marlene Dietrich, Diana Vreeland, Howard Hughes, Eleanor Roosevelt, and Gloria Vanderbilt, among many other celebrities.

Café Nicholson became a Manhattan "in" spot thanks to Lewis's cooking and charm. The *New York Times* notes that "restaurant critic Clementine Paddleford reviewed the restaurant in 1951 in the *New York Herald Tribune*, calling the soufflé 'light as a dandelion seed in a wind' and noting a sense of pride in the chef: 'We saw Edna peering in from the kitchen, just to see the effect on the guests and hear the echoes of praise.'" In reading this, we must keep in mind that women chefs were rare enough at that time, black women chefs unheard of.

In 1954, Lewis left the Café, partly at the request of her husband Steve Kingston, a Communist Party member and organizer, who objected to her feeding "the capitalists." Together they started a pheasant farm in New Jersey that failed. Eventually Lewis became chef at Gage & Tollner, a famous restaurant in Brooklyn she put back on the map as a fashionable stop for wealthy New Yorkers. She also worked as a volunteer at the American Museum of American History, which she loved. In 1972, she published her first cookbook, *The Edna Lewis Cookbook,* which was immediately praised by both James Beard and M. K. F. Fisher, the two best known food writers of the day. It was followed in 1976 by a second book, *The Taste of Country Cooking,* then in 1988 *In Pursuit of Flavor,* and in 2003, *The Gift of Southern Cooking,* with her student and friend Scott Peacock. *The Edna Lewis Cookbook* includes some non-Southern recipes but already introduces the idea of local ingredients and seasonal focus. *The Taste of Country Cooking* and *The Gift of Southern Cooking* are both considered high points of southern food history.

In 1990, Ms. Lewis received the Lifetime Achievement Award of the IACP (International Association of Culinary Professionals) and in 1995 the James Beard Foundation's Living Legend Award (their first such award). In her last years, she lived with Mr. Peacock in Atlanta and died, aged 89, in 2006.

Hunter Lewis

Some Notes on the Use of This Book

Our aim has been to present a cookbook with recipes for the kind of food that we feel people really eat and that are not too complicated to prepare. We have tried as much as possible to select ingredients that are generally available.

We have felt some concern that certain cuts of meat called for in the recipes are expensive by the pound, but in testing we found that this is often offset by the lack of waste in well-trimmed, prime meat.

The use of fresh ingredients of fine quality is as important to the final results of a recipe as is care in preparation. Good cooking and baking demand a considerable expenditure of time and effort, and we urge you to make the time and effort worthwhile by always using ingredients of the best quality.

Good cooking equipment is another important component of successful cooking. Saucepans and skillets should be heavy bottomed and sturdily made. We recommend those made of heavy aluminum, of copper lined with tin, or of stainless steel with cast aluminum bottoms, as these are all good conductors of heat. Our favorite dishes for casseroles are those made of enameled cast iron. A Pyrex double boiler is useful when you wish to keep something hot—a sauce Béarnaise for example—but do not want the water in the lower section to boil. And we have been devoted users of the KitchenAid food preparer (electric mixer) for years.

A stove with well-insulated ovens and burners that can be adjusted easily is important also. All of the recipes in this book were tested on a Garland range, which while designed for commercial cooking has become popular for home use because of its excellent, heavy construction. The burners are wide so that the heat extends to the edges of pots and pans, thus assuring even cooking, and they can be lowered sufficiently to permit cooking at a point just below a simmer, which is so important in the preparation of many dishes.

We would like to make a strong plea for the use of fresh herbs, as we feel they give interest and distinction to so many foods. With the addition of fresh herbs, a simply made blender mayonnaise, for example, becomes an exotic and savory sauce for seafood or cold chicken. A *poulet à la crème* is quite delicious with just a sprinkling of freshly cut parsley, but a sprinkling of fresh tarragon so enhances its taste and aroma that it becomes a dish special enough for any occasion.

Fresh herbs have become increasingly available; if you have a garden or a window sill, you can have them the year round. Potted herbs are on the market in early spring or can be ordered by mail at any time from many herb farms throughout the country.

We have not recommended specific wines for each menu, but we hope that you will serve and enjoy wine with all of them.

Most of the recipes were planned for four people. The exceptions are the buffet and Christmas dinners, which were planned to serve from ten to twelve.

We hope that this book will help you enjoy all the phases of cooking; and together we conclude that the most we could wish you is that you will find as much pleasure in cooking and tasting from the pages as we have had in putting them together.

Edna Lewis
Evangeline Peterson

Some Notes and Comments on Baking

We used unbleached, all-purpose flour for all the recipes in this book. We sensed possible chaos because of the present availability of so many different sizes of eggs, so unless otherwise specified we mean large eggs as contrasted to extra large and jumbo.

It's important to have all the ingredients used in baking at room temperature. There are some exceptions such as the shortening and water for pastry dough. When these exceptions occur, they are indicated in the recipes.

We recommend weighing flour rather than using cup measurements, especially in cake making. If the proportions of liquid and flour are not exact, cakes are likely to be heavy and coarse-textured. The only sure way we know of avoiding the hazard of adding too much flour (because flour packs down so easily, especially in the summer or on damp days, even when you measure with the greatest delicacy and care) is to use kitchen scales. If you don't have a scale, with a gentle touch spoon the flour into standard measuring cups and sift twice. Then sift a third and final time directly into the measuring cup and level it off with a knife.

In retesting the cookie recipes, we discovered that the use of extra-heavy cookie sheets eliminates the problem of cookies browning too quickly on the bottom before they are baked through. If you can't find extra-heavy cookie sheets, use two standard-weight sheets, one on top of the other. The caramel almond cookies were the one exception; these baked perfectly on a single standard-weight cookie sheet.

On Baking Pies and Tart Shells

Making a perfect pie with a tender, flaky crust is most satisfying. The suggestions that follow will, we hope, help you to achieve this happy result every time.

As in all baking, the ingredients must be fresh. The shortening should be chilled, the water cold, and the flour, salt, and sugar (when called for) sifted together to ensure even blending.

3

A simple, efficient means of cutting shortening into flour when making pie crust is the pastry blender. Another method that also gives excellent results is to chop the butter into the flour with a cook's knife. The butter should be almost frozen, then cut into small pieces. Place the flour in the center of a board, and scatter the pieces of butter over it. Chop with a fast, straight, chopping motion. When the mixture has the texture of cornmeal, sprinkle water over it quickly and then pull the dough together lightly with a fork.

If you are making a pie with a top and bottom crust, divide the dough carefully into two slightly unequal portions. If you have to reroll it, you will risk having a tough and lifeless crust.

All pie doughs should rest in the refrigerator for at least twenty minutes before they are rolled out. This makes the rolling-out process much easier. If as you roll out the dough the edges begin to split, let it stand a few minutes at room temperature until the dough is more pliable.

Be gentle but firm with the rolling pin, as pressing it too hard is another cause of hard, leathery pastry. Starting at the center, roll the dough away from you. Pick the dough up frequently and give it a quarter turn. If the dough sticks, stop to flour the undersurface.

Getting the rolled-out dough into the pie can be a problem for many people. An easy method we have found is to roll the crust up on a rolling pin, and then unroll it over the pie dish. This is an especially helpful technique when the crust is a very short one, such as the crust in the strawberry tart recipe.

We found glass pie dishes good for baking most pies, as the heat in glass cookware seems to produce a nicely browned and drier bottom crust.

It's our opinion that thickening agents spoil the flavor of fresh fruits. If you don't like runny pies, make small individual tarts.

It's essential that the first few minutes of baking take place in a hot oven (this is especially true of fruit pies) in order to assure a tender, flaky crust.

Fruit pies have the most flavor when served warm so plan to make them an hour or two before dinner. If you have any pie left over, reheat it for five to ten minutes in a hot oven just before serving.

A young Edna Lewis.

Spring Dinner Menus

Cold Poached Lobster with Special Sauce (p. 9)
Roast Rack of Spring Lamb with Herb Butter (p. 10)
Asparagus with Browned Bread Crumbs (p. 11)
Sautéed Potato Balls (p. 12)
Bibb Lettuce and Watercress Salad with French Dressing (p. 12)
French Bread
Assorted Cheeses
Baba Au Rhum with Whipped Cream and Strawberries (p. 13)
Coffee

Fresh Crabmeat with Light Mayonnaise (p. 15)
Sautéed Breasts of Chicken with Garnish of Mushrooms (p. 16)
Wild Rice (p. 17)
Green Beans with Parsley (p. 18)
Romaine Lettuce with Italian Watercress
French Bread
Profiterole Filled with Whipped Cream and Custard and
Served with Hot Chocolate Sauce (p. 19)
Coffee

Ragout of Lamb (p. 20)
New Potatoes
Boston Lettuce with French Dressing (p. 12)
Hot Buttered French Bread
Strawberry Tart (p. 21)
Coffee

Poulet À La Crème (p. 23)
White Rice (p. 24)
Mixed Green Salad with French Dressing (p. 12)
Fresh Strawberries in Lemon Juice
Sunday Night Cake (p. 24) or Caramel Almond Cookies (p. 25)
Coffee

Cold Poached Lobster
with Special Sauce

Lobster

- 3 1½-pound lobsters, very alive and active

Bouillon for Poaching

- 1 pint cold water
- 1 cup vermouth or dry white wine
- 2 slices onion
- Lemon slice
- 1 carrot, cut up
- 2 sprigs parsley
- ¼ teaspoon fresh thyme, or ¼ scant teaspoon dried

1. Place bouillon ingredients in a large pot about 10 inches wide and 4½ inches deep and bring to a boil. Cover the pot and let the bouillon simmer gently for 15 minutes before adding the lobsters.

Poaching the Lobsters

1. With a pair of tongs place the lobsters in the pot of boiling bouillon. Replace the lid quickly, as the lobsters will cool the stock. When the liquid begins to boil again, turn the burner low and let the lobsters simmer for 15 minutes.
2. Remove the pot from the burner, take off the lid, and let the lobsters cool in the stock.

3. When lobsters have cooled, take them from the pot and, with lobster or nut picks and poultry shears, pick out the meat. With a nutcracker crack open the claws and gently lift out the meat with a small fork. Next, break off the tail from the body and with the poultry shears split tail lengthwise. Take out the tail meat and remove the black string running down the back. Cut the meat into smaller pieces, place in a bowl, cover well, and refrigerate until serving time.
4. Serve the lobster on a bed of romaine lettuce with either special sauce or freshly made mayonnaise with herbs (page 15).

Special Sauce for Cold Lobster and Shrimp

- ½ cup tomato catsup
- 4 tablespoons dry sherry
- 3 tablespoons lemon juice
- 7 drops Tabasco
- 2 teaspoons fresh finely cut chives
- Pinch of salt

1. Combine ingredients, mix well, and keep in the refrigerator in a covered dish until ready to serve.

Roast Rack of Spring Lamb with Herb Butter

A rack of spring lamb is characterized by small rib bones and a small eye; the meat will be tender and the flavor delicate. When ordering the lamb, tell the butcher how many people you will be serving (allow 2 to 3 chops for each person). Ask him to "french" the bones, which involves scraping off any meat or fat 2 inches from the end of each bone, and to crack the ribs for easier carving.

Spring Lamb

- 1 to 2 racks spring lamb (about 2½ pounds each)
- 2 tablespoons soft butter
- Salt and pepper
- Watercress

1. Wipe the meat with a damp cloth and rub well with the soft butter. Set aside for at least one hour at room temperature.
2. To prevent the bones from burning during cooking, cover them with a pocket made of aluminum foil.
3. Sprinkle the lamb with salt and freshly ground pepper, place on a rack in a low-sided roasting pan, and roast for 35 to 40 minutes in a 425°F oven.
4. Remove the rack from the oven and spread the herb butter over the lamb. Place on a serving platter before carving into chops so that the melting herb butter and the juices from the lamb mingle and make a natural sauce. Garnish with watercress.

Herb Butter

- 2 tablespoons butter
- 1 teaspoon finely cut chives
- 1 teaspoon finely cut chervil

1. Cream the butter in a small dish with the back of a spoon and blend in well the finely cut chives and chervil.

Asparagus with Browned Bread Crumbs

Asparagus

꒰ **2 pounds asparagus**

1. Wash asparagus and break off the ends. They will snap off at the point where the brittle part ends. As the heads are usually gritty, clean by standing the stalks on their tips in a narrow vessel of water for about an hour. Standing them this way prevents them from absorbing water through the stalk ends.

2. Tie the cleaned asparagus in 3 to 4 bundles with white cotton string (this will make it easier to remove them from the cooker), and place upright in an asparagus cooker or in an inverted double boiler over boiling water. Cook for 8 to 10 minutes only.

3. Drain off the water and keep the asparagus covered until the butter-crumb sauce has been prepared, then place on a hot serving dish, cut and remove the strings, and pour the sizzling hot butter-crumb mixture over the asparagus. Serve immediately.

Browned Bread Crumbs

꒰ **3 tablespoons butter**
꒰ **1 tablespoon freshly made bread crumbs**

1. Place the butter in a small skillet and heat to the foaming stage. Sprinkle in bread crumbs and let brown for a minute before adding to the asparagus.

NOTE: Perfect bread crumbs are easily made in seconds by removing the crusts from a slice of bread and placing it in an electric blender.

Sautéed Potato Balls

———

- 6 large Idaho potatoes (about 3 pounds)
- ¾ stick butter
- salt

1. Peel the potatoes and shape out balls with a melon-ball scoop. Wash the balls in cold water and wrap in a damp linen towel until needed.

2. To cook the potatoes heat a heavy 9-inch skillet over medium to high heat. Bring the butter to the foaming stage and put in the potato balls. Cook at high heat, shaking the pan often so that the potatoes will brown evenly. They should be done in 12 to 13 minutes.

3. With a perforated spoon, dip them up onto a pan lined with paper toweling. Drain a minute, then spoon them into a serving dish and sprinkle lightly with salt.

French Dressing with Vinegar

———

- ¼ cup red wine vinegar
- ½ cup French olive oil
- ¼ teaspoon dry mustard
- 1 tablespoon grated new white potato
- ½ teaspoon freshly ground black pepper
- 1 teaspoon salt (pure salt crystals preferred)

1. Use a clean pint jar with a tight-fitting cover. Pour in the vinegar, dissolve the salt and mustard, and add the remaining ingredients.

2. Screw the top on securely, and shake vigorously until the mixture is thick and gray.

3. Shake again before dressing the salad greens, which should be done just before serving.

French Dressing with Lemon

- 3 tablespoons fresh lemon juice
- ⅓ cup French olive oil
- ¼ teaspoon dry mustard
- ¼ teaspoon pure salt
- ½ teaspoon freshly ground pepper

1. Prepare as previous dressing, but without adding the grated potato.

Baba au Rhum with Whipped Cream and Strawberries

For best results in baking with yeast, all utensils and ingredients should be warm. The dough will rise with the most satisfactory results if placed in a draft-free spot where the temperature is approximately 80°F. Too high a temperature will give a very yeasty taste while too low a temperature will cause the dough to rise too slowly, resulting in poor texture and flavor.

Baba

- 1 package dry yeast or ¾ yeast cake
- 2 teaspoons plus 2 tablespoons sugar
- 2 cups unsifted flour
- ½ cup lukewarm milk
- 1 teaspoon salt
- 3 eggs, lightly beaten
- 1½ sticks (6 ounces) sweet butter at room temperature
- ¼ cup slivered almonds (optional)

1. To make the baba, place the yeast, the two teaspoons of sugar, and two tablespoons of the flour in a 2-to-3-quart bowl and mix well. Sprinkle the lukewarm milk over it and set the bowl in a warm, draft-free place until the mixture becomes foamy, which will take about 15 to 20 minutes.

2. As soon as it reaches this stage mix in the other ingredients. Add the remaining flour, the lightly beaten eggs, and the salt, and stir well until the batter becomes smooth (about 5 minutes). Again, set the bowl in a warm place to allow the dough to rise and double in bulk. This will take about an hour.

3. Gently stir down the dough, add the softened butter and two tablespoons of sugar. Mix well and pour into a 9½" x 2½" ring mold that has been buttered and then dusted with flour; return mixture to the warm, sheltered spot until the dough rises to within ½ inch from the top of the mold, which will take from 20 to 30 minutes.

4. Allow 15 minutes to preheat the oven to 375°F. Set the mold carefully onto a cookie sheet and place in the middle rack of the oven for 25 minutes. Remove from the oven and let rest in the mold for 10 to 12 minutes.

5. Place a round platter over the baba, invert the mold, and remove the cake. Cover the baba with a light, clean cloth.

Rum Syrup

- ⅔ **cup granulated sugar**
- **1 cup water**
- **Lemon slice**
- ⅓ **cup dark Jamaican rum**

1. While the baba is baking, or as it cools, make the rum syrup. Place ⅔ cup of sugar, the lemon slice, and a cup of water in a saucepan and bring to a boil. Let simmer for about 12 minutes. Measure out ½ cup of the syrup (discard the rest) and stir in ⅓ cup of Jamaican rum.

2. About 1 hour before serving, spoon the hot rum syrup over the baba. The syrup must be hot in order to soak in properly. (If you like, you can at this point press slivered almonds onto the top and sides.)

Glaze

- **1 jar (12 ounces) apricot preserves**

1. Heat the apricot preserves slowly to the boiling point. Let them boil vigorously for a few minutes, then pour boiling hot over the baba. It is always interesting to see how beautifully the preserves adhere to the baba when it is poured this way, giving the baba a perfect glaze.

Whipped Cream Filling

- **1½ cups heavy cream**
- **Sugar to taste**
- **2 tablespoons rum or vanilla extract**
- **½ cup small whole or sliced strawberries**

1. Next, move the baba to a serving dish by sliding two wide spatulas under it. Fill the center with sweetened whipped cream and place whole strawberries around the edge. This is not a dessert to "place in the refrigerator until needed," so plan to serve it without delay!

Fresh Crabmeat with Light Mayonnaise

The delicate flavor of crabmeat is often lost under too spicy a sauce. A light mayonnaise made with lemon juice or tarragon-flavored white wine vinegar with fresh cut chervil added to it is subtle enough to enhance, and not mask, this delicate flavor. (If fresh chervil is not available, you may substitute a teaspoon of finely cut fresh parsley for each cup of mayonnaise.)

Crabmeat

- **1 pound fresh lump crabmeat**
- **Romaine lettuce**
- **1 cup light mayonnaise**
- **1 tablespoon finely cut fresh chervil**
- **Lemon wedges**

1. Pick over the crabmeat carefully to remove any bits of shell or cartilage. Arrange the crabmeat on beds of romaine lettuce on four individual serving dishes. Garnish each with a lemon wedge, and serve with the mayonnaise.

Light Mayonnaise

- **2 egg yolks**
- **½ teaspoon dry mustard**
- **1 teaspoon salt**
- **1½ cups olive oil**
- **1 tablespoon lemon juice and 1 tablespoon white wine vinegar, or 2 tablespoons of either one of these**
- **Pinch of cayenne pepper**

1. Place the egg yolks, mustard, and salt in a large mixing bowl. Beat well with a wire whisk for 1 or 2 minutes. Add the oil drop by drop, stirring all the while. When the mixture begins to thicken, alternate the oil with the vinegar or lemon juice. Continue to beat until the mayonnaise holds its own shape.

2. To make herb mayonnaise, add about 3 tablespoons of your favorite herb (or a combination of herbs) finely chopped, and mix into mayonnaise. Chervil, tarragon, chives, watercress, and parsley all enhance with their own special flavor and bouquet.

3. This recipe can also be made with excellent results in an electric blender and we actually prefer it made this way. Blenders produce a very light-textured mayonnaise, which is perfect for serving with cold poached chicken, lobster, and crabmeat.

4. Place all of the ingredients in the blender container except 1 cup of oil. Cover and turn the motor to high speed and blend for about 20 seconds. Uncover, and slowly pour in the remaining oil until the mayonnaise is thick. Blender mayonnaise will keep very well in the refrigerator, but it is at its best when served the same day it is made.

Sautéed Breasts of Chicken with Garnish of Mushrooms

This is my favorite way to serve breast of chicken, and I especially like it with wild rice. I often serve it just as is, or will sometimes add the cream sauce to it.

Chicken

- 4 chicken breasts, split, skinned, and boned
- ½ cup flour seasoned with salt and pepper
- ½ stick butter

1. Wipe the chicken breasts with a damp cloth. Shape them with your hands, then dip them in flour that has been seasoned with salt and pepper.

2. Place the floured pieces on a platter or sheet of waxed paper, and let them rest an hour or so to let the flour set well on the flesh.

3. To cook, heat a 10" skillet, add a half stick of butter, and as the peak of the foaming stage begins to subside, add the chicken breasts, plump side down. Cook over medium-high heat for 4 minutes and turn. Sauté 3 minutes on the flat side. Place the sautéed pieces of chicken in a hot, buttered casserole. Dot with thin pats of butter and place in a 325°F oven. This will safely hold the chicken without drying for as long as 15 minutes, and allows time to finish preparing the rest of the meal. Reserve the pan juices in the skillet for the sauce.

4. Add the mushrooms to the casserole, squeezing more lemon juice over the contents. If you are serving the chicken breasts without the cream sauce, sprinkle over some finely cut parsley.

Cream Sauce

- 1 pint heavy cream
- 3 tablespoons sweet sherry
- 2 teaspoons finely chopped fresh tarragon
- Nutmeg
- Salt and freshly ground pepper

1. To prepare the cream sauce, pour the heavy cream into a wide frying pan, place pan over medium heat and allow cream to boil rapidly until it is reduced by half or less (don't worry, it will not curdle). Add any juices that have collected in the bottom of the casserole. Stir in the sherry, the fresh tarragon cut fine (use only fresh tarragon, as dried tarragon just doesn't work; if you don't have it, substitute fresh parsley), salt, pepper, and a grating of nutmeg. Mix well and pour over the chicken.

Garnish of Sautéed Mushrooms

It is important to cook mushrooms over high heat, as this seems to seal in their moisture and keep them plump and firm. If the heat is too low, they will stew and become wrinkled and rubbery.

- ½ pound mushrooms of equal size
- 3 tablespoons butter
- ¼ lemon
- Finely chopped parsley
- Salt and freshly ground pepper to taste

1. Heat a small skillet, add the butter, and as the peak of the foaming stage begins to subside, add the mushrooms in a single layer. Sauté the mushrooms over high heat, shaking the pan back and forth as they cook, which will take about 4 to 5 minutes.

2. When the mushrooms are done, squeeze the lemon juice over them, add the salt, freshly ground pepper, and a sprinkling of parsley.

Wild Rice

- 3 cups wild rice
- 3 cups cold water
- Pinch of thyme
- Salt to taste
- 1 tablespoon butter

1. Wash the rice, removing any straw or chaff. Place in a saucepan and add 3 cups of cold water and a pinch of thyme.

2. Bring this to a boil and then turn the heat down as low as possible and let the rice barely simmer for 1 hour. After an hour, add salt and pepper according to your taste and a tablespoon of butter.

3. If you are serving the wild rice with chicken, use 1 cup of chicken stock in place of 1 cup of the water. If you are preparing roast chicken, substitute 1 tablespoon of the pan juices for the butter.

Green Beans with Parsley

- **3 pounds green beans**
- **3 teaspoons salt**
- **3 tablespoons butter**
- **Freshly cut parsley**

1. Pick over the green beans carefully, selecting only slender ones of equal size and discarding the overgrown ones. Wash, drain, and snip off the ends. When young, tender beans are not available, French-cut them with a bean slicer, which will make them both more tender and more attractive. It will also shorten the cooking time.

2. After the beans have been prepared, tie them with thin white cord into 6 to 8 bundles. This makes it easier to serve the beans more attractively. If you're not going to cook the beans right away, cover them with waxed paper and refrigerate.

3. To cook, fill a 3-quart saucepan three-fourths full with cold water and bring to a boil. Add the salt and the beans. The water will stop bubbling when you plunge in the beans, so cover the pan immediately until the water returns to a boil.

4. Let the beans boil rapidly, uncovered, for 12 minutes. Remove any scum that has risen to the surface, and drain off the water. Replace the lid and set in a warm spot.

5. Heat the butter until it foams, place the beans on a serving dish, cut and discard the cords, and pour the sizzling hot butter over the beans. Garnish with freshly cut parsley.

Profiterole Filled with Whipped Cream and Custard and Served with Hot Chocolate Sauce

Profiterole

- 1 cup milk
- 1 stick soft butter
- ½ tablespoon sugar
- 1 cup sifted flour
- 4 eggs
- ⅓ cup blanched slivered almonds (optional)

1. Preheat the oven to 425°F.
2. Sift the flour into a mixing bowl. Put the milk, butter, and sugar in a saucepan and let mixture come to a boil. Add the flour bit by bit until the batter is well mixed and smooth.
3. Add the eggs, one at a time, beating well after each addition until the mixture is again smooth
4. Using a small rounded spoon, drop by spoonfuls onto a cookie sheet, forming a 9" circular or 10" oval ring about 1" across and 1" high. (There will be enough batter left over to make 5 to 6 individual puffs.) The dough can also be piped onto the sheet with a cookie press. If you like the crunchiness of nuts, the ring can be sprinkled with slivered almonds.
5. Place in a 425°F oven for 25 to 30 minutes. To prevent the ring from collapsing, do not open the oven door for 25 minutes.
6. Remove the ring from the baking sheet and place it on a wire rack to cool. A half hour before serving, cut through the profiterole with a serrated bread knife, lay the top aside, and remove any moist dough from the center.
7. Fill the ring with the whipped cream into which you have folded ½ cup of custard sauce. Replace the top. Serve the profiterole with rich chocolate sauce.

Whipped Cream for Filling

- 1 cup heavy cream
- 2 teaspoons vanilla extract
- Sugar to taste

1. Whip the cream, sweeten to taste, and flavor with vanilla extract.

Custard Sauce (Pastry Cream)

- 1 cup milk
- ⅓ cup fine granulated sugar
- ½ vanilla bean
- 2 whole eggs plus 1 yolk
- 3 tablespoons cornstarch
- 1 tablespoon vanilla extract or brandy

1. Scald the milk with the vanilla bean and sugar until the sugar has dissolved.

2. Beat the eggs and mix in cornstarch well.

3. Remove the vanilla bean from the hot milk mixture, and slowly pour the milk into the blended eggs and cornstarch. Mix well and place in a double boiler over water that is barely simmering or over very low heat for 10 minutes, stirring all the while. Strain the sauce and cool.

4. When cool, flavor with vanilla extract or brandy.

Chocolate Sauce

- **1 cup light cream**
- **⅔ cup extra-fine sugar**
- **3 squares bitter chocolate**
- **1 teaspoon vanilla extract**

1. Melt the chocolate over hot water. Stir in the sugar. Scald the cream in a separate saucepan and stir into the chocolate-sugar mixture. Cook over medium heat until the sauce begins to boil. Lower the heat and let the sauce simmer, stirring often. Cook until it is smooth and thick. Remove the pan from the burner, and when the sauce has cooled, add the vanilla flavoring.

Ragout of Lamb

- **Half a leg of lamb (about 2 ½ pounds)**
- **Some lamb bones (including the bone from the leg)**
- **Bouquet garni of parsley, a bay leaf, and thyme**
- **1 medium-sized onion**
- **5 peppercorns**
- **1 quart cold water**
- **½ stick plus 2 tablespoons butter**
- **1 stalk celery, with leaves**
- **½ cup good dry white wine**
- **¼ teaspoon white pepper**
- **12 small white onions**
- **3 carrots, peeled and cut in 2" oval-shaped lengths**
- **¾ pound small mushrooms**
- **½ pound young green beans with ends snipped off**
- **Salt to taste**
- **1 tablespoon freshly cut parsley and chervil**

1. Have the butcher cut the pieces of meat from the leg in 1 ½" cubes, and ask for some extra lamb bones, including the one from the leg.

2. Make a stock by placing the bones in a quart of cold water, and add the bouquet garni of 1 or 2 sprigs of parsley, a bay leaf and thyme (fresh, if possible), then 1 onion and 5 peppercorns. Bring to a boil, and then reduce the heat so that the stock just simmers for about 2 hours or so. Strain and set to cool. When the stock has cooled, skim off all the fat that has risen to the surface.

3. Heat the half-stick of butter in a 12" heavy-bottomed skillet to the point just past the peak of the foaming stage, and add the lamb, 8 to 10 pieces at a time. Sauté well on all sides without browning too much, as too much browning destroys the delicate flavor of lamb. As the pieces are finished, spoon them into a 3-quart casserole.

4. When all the meat has been seared, add just enough of the defatted stock to cover the meat, then add the wine and the celery, including the leaves. Sprinkle in the ¼ teaspoon of white pepper and place the casserole on a low burner to simmer or in a 325°F preheated oven.

5. After 45 minutes sauté the carrots and the onions until they have lightly browned. In a separate skillet sauté the mushrooms. Add these to the casserole along with the green beans. If you enjoy the flavor of garlic with lamb, add a small minced clove.

6. Cook the ragout another 25 minutes or until the vegetables are tender.

7. Just before serving, add salt to taste and sprinkle with fresh parsley and chervil.

Strawberry Tart

Pastry

- 1 cup all-purpose flour, sifted
- ⅔ stick butter
- ¼ cup granulated sugar
- 1 egg yolk
- Pinch salt
- 1 teaspoon vanilla

1. To make the pastry, place the ingredients in a medium-sized bowl. Mix together with your fingertips until you have a soft, granular dough. Shape it lightly into a round cake and place it in the refrigerator to rest no more than 20 minutes. If it chills longer than this, it will become too firm and will split along the edges when it is rolled out.

2. Roll the dough on a lightly floured board or pastry cloth with a cold, lightly floured rolling pin. This is a fragile dough and needs to be handled quickly. To prevent it from sticking, stop frequently to gently lift the dough from the board and give it a quarter turn.

3. Roll out to a thickness of 1/16" to 1/8". To gauge the size, place a 9" false-bottom or layer-cake pan on the rolled-out dough and allow an additional inch for the sides.

4. To place the dough in the tart pan, roll it up onto the pin and carefully unroll it over the pan. Lightly shape it into the bottom and sides. Don't be concerned if the dough comes apart in places as you handle it. Once in the pan, it is easily mended by pressing it together lightly

with your fingertips along the top edge of the pan. Pierce the bottom and sides of the crust with a table fork.

5. Bake in a 360°F oven for 20 to 25 minutes. After about 12 minutes, check the tart shell. If it is puffing up, pierce it again but without letting the tines go all the way through. When the pastry has reached an overall light brown, remove it from the oven and set it on a rack to cool.

6. To remove the tart shell from the pan, place the pan on a cylindrical container such as a coffee tin or salt box smaller in circumference than the pan itself. Press down gently on the ring and it should easily slide off. The false bottom can remain under the tart, or the tart can be eased off onto a serving plate with the aid of a spatula.

Filling

- 10 ounces strawberry preserves, pressed through a sieve
- 1 quart fresh strawberries, washed, hulled, and dried
- ⅔ cup heavy cream
- 2 tablespoons sugar
- 2 teaspoons vanilla or Grand Marnier

1. Press the strawberry preserves through a medium sieve. Paint the bottom and sides of the cooled crust with a light coat of this mixture.

2. Fill the tart with whole strawberries, arranging them in one or more layers according to the size of the berries.

3. Heat the unused preserves to boiling, and glaze the berries by spooning ¼ teaspoonful—just enough to cover—over each berry.

4. Whip the cream, sweeten with the sugar, and flavor with the vanilla or Grand Marnier. Place the whipped cream in the refrigerator until needed.

5. Before serving, garnish the tart with a ring of whipped cream piped or spooned around the outer edge; or serve the cream separately.

Poulet à la Crème

- 1 2¼-to-3-pound chicken, cut into eight pieces
- 2 tablespoons butter
- 6 to 8 small white onions
- ¼ pound mushrooms
- 3 small carrots, sliced
- 2 sprigs parsley
- 1 bay leaf
- 2 cloves
- ½ cup dry white wine or dry vermouth
- 1 teaspoon salt
- ¾ cup heavy cream
- 2 teaspoons finely chopped fresh tarragon
- Wash and pat dry the pieces of chicken

1. Heat a 10" skillet over moderately high heat and add the butter. When the foaming stage begins to subside add the chicken, 4 pieces at a time, and sauté quickly without browning over high heat. This initial step is called "seizing"; and what it does is to firm the skin, which keeps it from shriveling up or shrinking, so that the chicken will appear attractive and appetizing when it is served. As the pieces are finished, place them in a 2-quart casserole or saucepan.

2. Next, stick one of the onions with the 2 cloves, and stir in the onions, sliced carrots, mushrooms, parsley, and bay leaf.

3. Add the ½ cup of white wine or vermouth.

4. Place the casserole on a burner, and after the liquid comes to a gentle boil, lower the heat so that the chicken simmers for about 45 minutes; or place the casserole in a 325°F oven for the same length of time.

5. Add the teaspoon of salt about 20 minutes before the chicken is cooked.

6. Reduce the cream by letting it boil up hard to about one half and add it to the casserole. Remove the bay leaf, and taste the sauce for seasoning. Add the chopped fresh tarragon and serve. If fresh tarragon is not available, use parsley, but don't substitute dried tarragon for fresh.

White Rice

After trying many different methods, I have found that the best way to cook rice that is dry and fluffy and with firm separate grains is to cook it very slowly over very low heat and with less water than is generally specified. The following recipes for two different types of rice always seem to give perfect results.

- 1 cup long-grain rice
- 1 cup cold water

or

- 1 cup parboiled rice
- 1½ cups cold water

1. Place the rice in a 2-quart saucepan with a tight-fitting cover, add the water, cover, and set over medium high heat to bring the rice quickly to a full boil. Immediately turn the heat very low to cook just under a simmer. Cook for 45 minutes.
2. The rice can be fluffed once halfway through cooking time with a two-pronged fork.
3. When cooked, rice can be kept for one to two hours in the top part of a double boiler over hot—but not boiling—water without losing its dry, firm texture.

Sunday Night Cake

Cake

- 1 stick butter (4 ounces)
- 1½ cups fine granulated sugar
- 3 medium eggs
- 2 cups minus 2 tablespoons all-purpose flour
- 3 teaspoons baking powder
- ¼ teaspoon (scant) salt
- ⅔ cup milk
- 1 tablespoon vanilla extract

1. Remove the milk, eggs, and butter from the refrigerator in time for them to be at room temperature before you begin to mix the cake batter.
2. Preheat the oven to 375°
3. Sift the flour twice, measure, then sift once again, adding the baking powder and salt.
4. Cream the butter until it has a satiny appearance (if you are using an electric mixer, beat at medium-low speed). Add the sugar gradually until it is well blended, then add the eggs one at a time, mixing in well.
5. Add the flour in three parts alternately with the milk, beginning and ending with

the flour. Mix well after each addition, but only to the point where the batter is blended.

6. Add the vanilla extract, and give a quick beat by hand, or for one or two seconds with a mixer at high speed.

7. Spoon the batter into a 9" x 9" x 1¾" cake pan with a buttered and flour-dusted bottom and place in the center of the middle rack of the oven.

8. After 35 minutes, test the cake to see if it is completely baked. Do this by inserting a toothpick or a cake tester, which will come out clean if the cake is done. Another way to test for doneness that I have found to be very reliable is to place your ear close to the surface of the cake; if you hear quiet bubbling, the batter is not completely baked and the cake should be returned to the oven for a few more minutes.

9. When you remove the cake from the oven, slide a thin knife around the edges, place a cake rack over the pan, and invert the pan.

10. After the cake has cooled for 15 minutes, cover with a clean cloth to prevent hardening of the surface and drying of the cake. Wait an hour before adding the following glaze.

Brown Sugar Glaze

- 1 cup packed brown sugar
- 3 tablespoons cold water

1. Place the sugar and water in a saucepan over a medium flame and let boil until it reaches the soft ball stage (230°F). Do not stir at any point during the cooking, but remove any scum that comes to the surface.

2. As soon as the soft ball stage is reached, remove the pan from the burner and place in a pan of ice water.

3. When the glaze becomes thick enough to spread, smooth over the cake with a narrow spatula or dinner knife.

Caramel Almond Cookies

- ¾ cup firmly packed brown sugar
- 3 tablespoons dark corn syrup
- 2 tablespoons butter
- ½ teaspoon cinnamon
- ½ cup all-purpose flour
- ⅔ cup coarsely chopped almonds
- Sweet butter

1. Preheat the oven to 400°F.

2. Place all the ingredients in a bowl and mix by hand until the mixture is pastey enough to hold together.

3. Pinch off enough dough to form small balls of a size that would fit into a ¼ teaspoon measure. Place them at least 3 inches apart on cookie sheets that have been generously rubbed with sweet butter.

4. Bake 5 to 7 minutes until the center appears like the edge: that is, the entire surface is bubbly.

5. Remove from the oven and slam the cookie sheet onto a table or counter top smartly with a firm bang. This is necessary to stop the bubbling. Let the cookies harden a minute or two, and then remove them quickly with a very thin spatula and place on a wire rack.

6. If some of the cookies stick to the sheet and cannot be removed, return the tin to the oven for a minute or two.

Edna Lewis in 1949, age 33.

Summer Dinner Menus

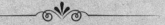

Prosciutto with Slices of Cantaloupe (p. 31)
Herb-Broiled Chicken with Grilled Mushrooms (p. 31)
Artichokes Vinaigrette (p. 32)
French Bread
Deep-Dish Blackberry Pie with Blackberry Sauce (p. 33)
Coffee

Gazpacho (p. 35)
Veal Scallops Sautéed with Lemon Sauce (p. 36)
Garnish of Sautéed Mushrooms (p. 17)
White Rice (p. 24)
Fresh Buttered Spinach (p. 37)
Meringue Torte (p. 38)
Coffee

Southern Fried Chicken (p. 41)
Corn on the Cob (p. 42)
Salad of Fresh Summer Greens with French Dressing (p. 12)
Hot Biscuits Split, Buttered, and Sugared with
Fresh Strawberries and Whipped Cream (p. 43)
Coffee

Prosciutto with Slices of Cantaloupe

You will need two slices of prosciutto for each serving. Select a ripe cantaloupe, peel and cut in half. Remove the seeds and cut the melon in slices about ¼" thick. Place the slices on leaves of romaine lettuce and cover with the prosciutto.

Herb-Broiled Chicken with Grilled Mushrooms

Herb-Broiled Chicken

- 2 chickens, 2½ pounds each, split in half
- 1 stick soft butter
- 1 small onion, sliced
- 1 sprig finely chopped tarragon
- ¼ lemon
- ¼ pound mushrooms for garnish
- Salt and grated pepper

1. Wash the chicken halves under cold water and dry well. Paint them over with softened butter and sprinkle with salt and grated pepper.
2. Place the chickens skin side down on a wire rack in a buttered pan. Put a few slices of onion in the cavities and sprinkle with finely chopped tarragon and a few drops of lemon juice.
3. Clean the mushrooms and remove the stems, then place them in the bottom of the broiler pan.
4. Broil the chickens about 5 inches below the heat for 20 minutes, basting occasionally with the juices in the pan.
5. Turn the chicken halves over, baste, and broil 25 minutes longer, continuing to baste until 10 minutes before removing them from the broiler.
6. Place the chickens on a hot serving platter and garnish with the mushrooms. Serve immediately while the skin is crisp and the meat is juicy. Don't allow broiled chicken to wait before serving or the skin will turn soggy and the meat will dry out.

Artichokes Vinaigrette

Artichokes

- 4 globe artichokes
- 3 teaspoons lemon juice
- 3 teaspoons salt
- 6 quarts boiling water

1. To prepare artichokes, remove the first layer of outer leaves, cut off the stems flush with the base, and cut off 1" from the tops.

2. Open up the leaves with your fingers so that you can remove the choke, which you will find in the center of the artichoke just above the base. Its fibrous, silky appearance makes the choke easy to spot. Dig it out with a sharply pointed spoon, taking care to remove it all.

3. Close the leaves back together, and to keep them tightly closed while the artichoke cooks, tie white string around the middle of each.

4. Place the artichokes in the boiling water, and add the lemon juice and salt. Cover, and keep the water at a lively boil. After 15 minutes, test by pulling a leaf. If it pulls out easily, the artichokes are done; if not, continue cooking a few minutes longer.

5. When they are cooked, remove them with a large slotted spoon and place them upside down to drain on a rack that has been placed over a bowl.

6. When they have cooled, remove them to a dish, cover, and set in a cool place or in the refrigerator. Lightly spoon vinaigrette sauce over them about a half hour before serving.

Vinaigrette Sauce

- ⅓ cup lemon juice
- ⅔ cup olive oil
- 1 teaspoon finely cut chervil (omit if fresh is not available)
- 1 teaspoon finely cut parsley
- ½ teaspoon dry mustard
- ½ teaspoon grated onion
- Salt to taste
- Freshly ground black pepper

1. Dissolve the salt and mustard in the lemon juice. Combine all ingredients well in a clean jar with a tight cover and shake. Shake again before using.

Deep-Dish Blackberry Pie
with Blackberry Sauce

Pie Crust

- 2 cups all-purpose flour
- ⅛ teaspoon salt
- 1½ sticks butter (6 ounces)
- ⅓ cup cold water

1. Place the flour, salt, and chilled butter (cut into small pieces) in a bowl and cut with a pastry blender until the mixture has the texture of cornmeal. Use a firm, chopping motion with the blender, rotating the bowl slowly with your left hand. Stop to clean off the blades of the blender if they become heavily coated.

2. Sprinkle the cold water quickly over the surface, mix with a large spoon, and pull the dough together lightly. Gently shape it into a ball with your fingers and then divide it into 2 slightly unequal portions. Place the dough in the refrigerator for 20 to 30 minutes before rolling. (For greater ease in rolling, chill the rolling pin as well.)

3. Remove the dough about 15 to 20 minutes before rolling it out, so that it will soften and be easy to handle.

4. Allow 15 minutes to preheat the oven to 450°F.

5. Lightly flour the rolling pin and board, and roll out the larger half into a square shape. To gauge the size, place an 8" x 8" x 2" Pyrex dish on the rolled-out dough and allow an additional 2½" all around to cover the sides and rim.

6. Roll up the dough onto the pin and carefully unroll it over the pie dish. Gently shape it into the bottom and sides of the dish.

7. If you are not going to fill and bake the pie immediately, cover it with waxed paper and return it to the refrigerator.

8. The top crust can also be rolled out in advance of baking and kept in the refrigerator between two sheets of waxed paper.

Filling

- 3 pints blackberries
- 1 cup sugar
- 5 thin pats chilled sweet butter

1. Sprinkle half of the sugar over the bottom crust and add the berries and the remaining sugar. Then dot the berries with the butter pats.

2. Roll the top crust into an 8" square.

3. With a pastry brush, moisten the edges of the bottom crust with cold water and place the top crust over the berries, unrolling it off the pin. Press down lightly along the rim with your fingertips and, using kitchen shears, trim off any excess dough. Make depressions around the rim with the dull edge of a knife.

4. Make several vents in the top crust before placing the pie on the middle rack in the preheated 450°F oven for 10 minutes. Then, after 10 minutes, lower the heat to 425°F for 35 minutes.

5. Serve the pie warm by itself, or with blackberry sauce and whipped cream.

Blackberry Sauce

- **1 pint blackberries**
- **½ cup sugar**

1. Take a handful from the pint of blackberries and crush them with a potato ricer or fork on the bottom of a saucepan. Add the remaining berries and sugar, and let this simmer gently about 15 minutes over medium-low heat.

2. Press through a sieve or a food mill and serve warm.

Gazpacho

Gazpacho

- 5 firm ripe tomatoes, peeled, quartered, and seeded
- 2 medium cucumbers, peeled, quartered, and seeded
- 1 green pepper, seeded and coarsely cut
- 1 or more cloves of garlic
- 3 tablespoons lemon juice
- 1 tablespoon red wine vinegar
- ¾ teaspoon freshly grated pepper
- 1½ teaspoons salt, or to taste
- ½ tablespoon soy sauce
- ½ cup olive oil
- 1 cup cold water
- 1 tablespoon chopped chervil or sweet basil (if available)
- 2 tablespoons sweet red onion, finely sliced

1. Mix all of the above ingredients, except for the freshly sliced red onion, together in a bowl, and spoon small amounts into an electric blender, blending only to the point at which the mixture is thick and still crunchy.

2. Taste for seasoning, and add the onions before placing in the refrigerator to chill for a few hours before serving.

Garnish

- ½ cup diced cucumber
- 1 to 2 cups croutons
- Garlic slice (optional)

1. Just before serving, stir in a half cup of diced cucumber. With the gazpacho, pass hot croutons that have been fried in butter with a slice of garlic (if you like the flavor).

NOTE: I make this without stock or broth as I find that they tend to mask the fresh flavor of summer vegetables.

Veal Scallops Sautéed
with Lemon Sauce

Ask the butcher for veal slices cut from the top of the round (which comes from the top of the leg). Slices from this section will have an attractive oval shape and, more important, will have no bone or gristle, which makes them ideal for quick sautéing. The meat should be light gray in color, an indication that it is milk-fed baby veal. This cut of veal is most likely to be found in a European-style butcher shop. For veal scallops, though you pay by the pound, it's best to order by the slice. Eight slices in this case would come to about 1¼ to 1½ pounds.

- **8 thin veal scallops pounded to ⅛" thickness**
- **½ cup flour**
- **1 teaspoon salt**
- **½ teaspoon pepper**
- **¾ stick butter plus ½ stick**
- **1½ lemons, freshly squeezed**

1. Season the flour with salt and pepper and spread on a platter. Press each slice of veal into the seasoned flour, shake off the excess flour, and place on a sheet of waxed paper.

2. Let the veal slices rest about an hour so that the flour will set well into the meat. If you don't have the hour to spare, you can get the same result by placing the dusted veal slices between sheets of waxed paper, and pounding them with a heavy mallet. It is important that the flour adhere as firmly as possible to the meat. Otherwise, if you sauté the veal immediately after dredging without either letting the meat rest or pounding the flour in, a certain amount of loose flour will fall off the meat and burn immediately in the butter. This will spoil the flavor of the butter sauce you will later use to garnish the finished dish.

3. Heat the butter to the foaming stage in a large heavy-bottomed skillet, and put in as many pieces of veal as the pan will hold. After a few minutes of cooking, the veal will shrink a bit, and you will be able to add another slice. Keep the pan as hot as you can but do not allow the butter to burn.

4. Cook the veal about 3 to 4 minutes on each side and remove to a warm platter while you finish cooking the remaining pieces.

5. Remove the pan from the heat and pour into it any juices that have drained onto the platter. Add the lemon juice and about 2 tablespoons of water.

6. Return the pan to the stove and cook over very high heat until the sauce thickens to a syrupy consistency and has a rich brown color. Spoon the sauce over each slice of veal.

NOTE: It's important that you not overcook the sauce, for if you do and it cooks beyond the syrupy stage, it will turn into oil and, because of the evaporation of the liquid, cannot be brought back to its former texture.

Fresh Buttered Spinach

- **3 to 4 pounds fresh spinach**
- **1½ sticks butter**

1. To prepare the spinach, first pick off the leaves and discard the stems. Wash the leaves in a large quantity of cold water, changing the water until no trace of sand appears in the bottom of the container. This thorough washing is essential, as gritty spinach can spoil the entire meal!

2. After the spinach has been thoroughly washed, spread the leaves out on toweling to drain well and dry, shuffling them from time to time.

3. To cook the spinach, place the butter in a heavy skillet and bring it to the foaming stage. Fill the pan with as much spinach as you can crowd in. With 2 large spoons, keep turning the spinach until it has wilted enough to allow room for the remaining leaves.

4. Keep the pan over high heat during the entire cooking time, and continue turning the leaves to keep them from burning.

5. If the heat is lowered, the spinach will stew instead of wilting. After about 10 minutes, the spinach should be cooked and the leaves shiny and very bright green in appearance.

NOTE: Cooking spinach is similar to cooking mushrooms. High heat helps these vegetables retain their moisture, whereas low heat will result in wrinkled and tough rather than succulent and tender vegetables.

Also, fresh spinach with the roots still attached is always preferable to the prepackaged "washed" variety.

Meringue Torte

This delicious dessert consists of 3 different parts: a cake, a custard filling, and a meringue topping. Any one, or all three, can be made a day in advance, leaving only the fun of putting them together a short time before serving.

For this summer menu, we have suggested garnishing the torte with fresh sliced peaches and raspberries, but many other fruits also combine well with this dessert—strawberries, cherries, or in fall or winter you might try diced fresh pineapple, sliced bananas with fresh orange segments, or any of the summer fruit that has been frozen and thawed.

According to the fruits you choose, you may also like to vary the flavoring of the custard and use a liqueur such as kirsch or a good dark rum.

The Cake for the Base

- ½ stick butter
- 1 cup all-purpose flour
- 1 cup extra-fine sugar
- ¼ teaspoon salt
- 5 egg whites (1 cup)
- 5 egg yolks
- 2 teaspoons vanilla extract

1. Cut the butter into small pieces on a sheet of waxed paper and place it in the freezer for about 15 minutes to harden.

2. Preheat the oven to 350°F.

3. Sift and measure the flour, then measure the sugar and add to it the ¼ teaspoon salt. Separate the eggs.

4. Spread out about half the flour on a cutting board. Remove the frozen butter from the refrigerator and place it on the flour. With a wide-bladed knife, chop the butter into the flour until it has a fine, even texture. Chop quickly, so that the butter doesn't soften and become sticky. Add the remaining flour and blend in the same way. Refrigerate this mixture until you are ready to fold it into the beaten eggs.

5. Place the egg yolks and sugar in a mixing bowl and beat (an electric mixer is fine for this) about 5 minutes at medium speed, until the mixture is pale in color and light in texture. Add the vanilla.

6. In a separate bowl, beat the egg whites until the peaks just begin to stiffen.

7. Partially fold the beaten yolks into the egg whites. Remove the butter-flour mixture from the refrigerator and add it to the beaten eggs by spoonfuls, continuing the folding motion with a large flat spoon or a rubber spatula just to the point where the mixture is well blended. (The egg whites will break down if you mix any more than is necessary.)

8. Fill a 9" layer-cake pan with a bottom three-fourths full. Place it on the middle shelf of the preheated oven for 45 minutes. When done, the cake should spring back when touched in the center.

9. Remove the cake from the oven and let it cool for about 15 minutes. Run a knife around the side of the pan, then set the pan on top of a coffee tin or a similar object that is smaller in diameter than the pan itself. With a quick, firm downward pressing, the rim should slide off. To remove the bottom of the pan, place a cake rack upside down over the cake and quickly invert the two together. Slide a thin knife between the cake and the bottom and lift off the disc. Don't bother to invert the cake again, as you'll be spreading the filling over this side of the cake.

10. Cover the cake lightly with a napkin or linen dish towel and let cool on the rack for about an hour.

The Custard Filling

- 1 cup light cream
- 3 tablespoons flour, sifted
- ⅓ cup granulated sugar
- Pinch of salt
- 3 egg yolks
- 2 tablespoons brandy
- ½ vanilla bean

1. Mix together well the flour, sugar, and salt in a saucepan. Pour in the light cream and add the vanilla bean. Cook over medium heat, stirring continuously with a wire whisk for 4 or 5 minutes. Remove from heat.

2. Lightly beat the yolks and stir in one-fourth of the hot cream mixture to warm the eggs. Add the eggs to the remaining hot cream, stirring briskly. Place the saucepan over a low flame and, stirring

constantly, cook only until the sauce is heated through.

3. Remove from the stove. Strain the custard through a fine sieve. Cover it lightly and set to cool. When cool, flavor with the brandy.

NOTE: If made in advance, cover well and store in the refrigerator. Remove the custard an hour or so before assembling the torte as it will have more flavor at room temperature and will spread more easily. Stir it well before spreading it over the cake.

The Meringue Topping

- 3 egg whites (½ cup)
- ½ cup extra-fine sugar
- ¼ cup hazelnuts in the skin, finely chopped
- ¼ teaspoon vanilla
- Few drops of almond extract

1. Preheat the oven to 250°F.

2. Separate the eggs and measure the sugar.

3. Chop the nuts on a board with a chef's knife. It is easier to chop a few nuts at a time, as they tend to scatter if you do them all at once. Measure them after chopping, and set them aside while you whip the whites. (It is not necessary to remove the skins from the hazelnuts; in addition to giving some color to the meringue, they also add flavor.)

4. Whip the egg whites in an open, shallow bowl with a wire whisk, using an elliptical motion. After 4 to 5 minutes of beating, they will stand in soft peaks. At this point, begin adding the sugar, a teaspoon at a time, while continuing to beat (about 4 minutes). Add the vanilla and the almond extract. Beat another 3 to 4 minutes or until the whites are stiff.

5. If you prefer using an electric mixer, follow the manufacturer's instructions for whipping egg whites. Just after the whites are foamy and are beginning to stiffen, gradually add the sugar and the extracts. When the whites are stiff, remove them from the mixer.

6. Sprinkle the nuts over the beaten whites, and lightly blend them in with 3 or 4 quick folds.

7. Spoon the mixture onto the removable bottom of a 9" cake pan (the same size used for the cake base). Set in the center of the middle rack of the oven.

8. After 1 hour turn off the heat. Leave the meringue in the oven for an additional hour, then remove and place in a draft-free spot to cool.

NOTE: This is not a dry, crispy meringue; it is crisp around the edges, yet chewy and moist inside. It can be made a day ahead and stored in a tin or well wrapped (though not closely) in waxed paper and foil. If the meringue softens, place it in a 350°F oven for a few minutes.

Assembling the Torte

1. Place the cake on a serving dish and spread over the custard filling. Cover with a layer of thinly sliced peaches and a scattering of fresh raspberries.

2. Carefully place the meringue on top.

3. Garnish the cake with a circle of sliced peaches placed around the edge of the cake.

4. Use a serrated knife to cut the cake, and slice with a light sawing motion.

Southern Fried Chicken

Fried chicken was considered a special dish in Virginia, because until the nineteen-twenties frying chickens—like lamb—were available only in the late spring and early summer; hence the term "spring chicken." They had a flavor rarely found today, perhaps because they were handfed with a feed of the farmer's own mixture.

The first spring chickens were pan-broiled, as they were too delicate to fry. A broiler weighed about 1 pound and was split once down the back, bathed in butter, seasoned, and carefully pan-broiled. When chickens grew to 1½ or 2 pounds, they were fried, and became even more popular than broilers, first as a breakfast meat and then as a special treat to be served at outdoor picnics and ball games.

Chicken

- 2 chickens, 2½ pounds each (cut in serving pieces)
- 1 cup shortening, lard, or butter
- 1 cup all-purpose flour
- 1 cup whole-wheat flour
- 3 teaspoons salt
- 1 teaspoon freshly ground black pepper
- ¾ stick butter (if shortening or lard is used)
- Freshly cut parsley

1. Combine the two flours, add the salt and pepper, and mix well. Roll the pieces of chicken in the seasoned flour, and place them in a layer on a platter or pan. Let them rest for 2 hours before cooking to allow time for the flour to adhere thoroughly to the chicken. This will make for crisp, evenly browned pieces.

2. To fry the chicken, heat the fat in the pan until a drop of water sizzles when flicked in. Place the chicken pieces in the pan. If shortening or lard is being used for frying, drop three-fourths of a stick of butter cut into small pieces over the chicken.

3. If all butter is used for frying, first heat the skillet, then bring the butter to the foaming stage. When it just begins to subside, place the chicken in the pan.

4. Cover the pan and continue to cook at fairly high heat. After 10 minutes, turn the chicken over, replace the cover, and cook another 10 minutes. If you want a deeper color, turn the chicken over once again; the total cooking time, however, should not be more than 25 minutes.

5. Remove the chicken to a warm serving platter and garnish with cut parsley. Serve piping hot.

Gravy for Southern Fried Chicken

- 4 chicken backs
- ½ medium onion
- ½ piece celery

- 🌿 **2 cups cold water**
- 🌿 **3 tablespoons flour**
- 🌿 **Salt and pepper**

1. If you like gravy with fried chicken, prepare a stock in advance with the chicken backs, onion, celery, and water. Simmer for 1 hour, strain, and set aside.

2. While the chicken is cooking, dip out 3 tablespoons of the fat from the chicken pan into an 8" skillet. Stir in flour and brown to a good color. Add enough of the chicken stock to make a gravy the thickness of heavy cream, and season with salt and pepper. Simmer until ready to serve.

3. If the gravy thickens too much, thin with some of the remaining stock. The special advantage of this gravy is that it can be served the minute the chicken is ready.

Corn on the Cob

An essential ingredient to tasty corn on the cob is its freshness. Ideally, corn should be picked just before cooking, but when this is not possible, try to buy corn that has been picked at dawn and then refrigerated.

1. Shuck the corn and place it in a kettle with cold water to cover.

2. Bring it to a full boil, and remove the kettle from the heat.

3. Corn cooked this way will be crisp and yet tender, and can remain in the water for as long as an hour without the kernels wrinkling up or getting soggy.

4. This method of cooking corn was told to us some summers ago by Norman Ives, an artist and a fine amateur cook. We found it to be a wonderful discovery that eliminated the frustration of watching perfectly cooked corn turn cold or shriveled before it was eaten.

5. Leave the corn in the kettle until the very moment your guests are ready, then lift out the exact number needed with a pair of tongs and relax, knowing that if toward the end of the meal someone wants more corn you can continue to serve flawless ears until everyone has had his fill or until you have run out of corn!

Hot Biscuits, Split, Buttered, and Sugared with Fresh Strawberries and Whipped Cream

This is our favorite kind of shortcake. It always seems just the appropriate base, too, for wild strawberries if you are lucky enough to be in an area where they grow.

- ¼ cup granulated sugar
- 2 cups flour
- 3 teaspoons baking powder
- ½ scant teaspoon salt
- 1 stick butter
- ⅔ cup milk
- 1 tablespoon melted butter
- 1½ pints fresh strawberries crushed with ½ cup sugar
- ½ pint heavy cream, whipped, sweetened to taste, and flavored with vanilla

1. Preheat oven to 450°F. Sift the flour, measure it carefully, and sift a second time with the salt and baking powder.

2. Place the flour mixture and the sugar in a mixing bowl. Add the shortening and blend well with a pastry blender or with your fingertips. Pour in all the milk and stir well with a wooden spoon.

When the dough has been thoroughly mixed, spoon it out onto a lightly floured board and knead it for a few seconds in order to gather it easily into a ball.

3. Pinch off the dough and shape by hand into 3" rounds about ¼" thick. (The dough can also be rolled to ¼" thickness, and cut with a biscuit cutter.)

4. Place the rounds on a cookie sheet and brush the tops with melted butter. Pierce them with a fork and place in the preheated oven for 12 to 15 minutes or until lightly browned.

5. Slice the biscuits in half with a bread knife. Spread each half with soft butter and sprinkle with a teaspoon of sugar.

6. Spoon a generous helping of the crushed strawberries over the bottom half of each biscuit. Cover with the top half and top with a generous dollop of whipped cream. Garnish with whole berries.

The backyard garden of the Café Nicholson in Manhattan, where Edna Lewis became cook and co-owner with Johnny Nicholson in 1949. Edna's innovative cooking quickly established Café Nicholson as one of New York's fashionable hotspots, evidenced by this photo taken soon after the restaurant opened. Authors Tennessee Williams and Gore Vidal can be seen seated on the right.

Outdoor Summer Menus

Charcoal-Grilled Lamb Chops (p. 47)
Ratatouille (p. 47)
Hot Buttered French Bread
Sunday Night Cake (p. 24)
Basket of Peaches, Plums, and Cherries
Coffee

Charcoal-Grilled Steak (Sauce Béarnaise Optional) (p. 48)
Braised Leeks (p. 50)
Fresh Tomato Slices
Hot Buttered French Bread
Fresh Peach Cobbler with Nutmeg Sauce (p. 50)
Coffee

Charcoal-Grilled Lamb Chops

The combination of charcoal-grilled lamb and ratatouille is one of our favorites, and, happily, it's an easy as well as delicious summer meal to prepare.

1. Purchase either loin or rib chops and have them cut about 2" thick, so that they can be well crisped outside and pink and juicy inside.

2. Use briquets made from hardwood charcoal such as hickory or oak for outdoor grilling. Spread the charcoal over an area large enough to cook the chops. Light the fire 30 minutes in advance, so that all the coals will be burning and covered with a light layer of ash when you cook the lamb.

3. The length of time needed for grilling the chops will depend on such variables as the heat of the fire, the amount of wind, and the type of grill used. In general, grill 2" chops between 15 and 25 minutes over a moderate fire depending on whether you like lamb cooked medium-rare or medium. Season the chops with salt and black pepper and arrange them on a hot platter with a garnish of watercress.

Ratatouille

This Mediterranean vegetable stew is a marvelous dish to make during the summer months, as it reheats well and is delicious served cold as a first course or as a relish.

- **2½ medium onions, coarsely grated**
- **5 tomatoes, peeled, seeded, and chopped**
- **2 small zucchini, thinly sliced**
- **1 medium to large eggplant, peeled, quartered, and coarsely chopped**
- **½ cup oil**
- **Freshly ground pepper**
- **Salt to taste**

1. Sauté the onion until it is transparent, then add the tomatoes and cook for about 15 minutes at a very slow simmer.

2. Add the zucchini and eggplant, grind in lots of black pepper, and simmer 3 to 4 hours. If you prefer, this dish can also cook well in a 325°F oven; after sautéing the onions and tomatoes, place all the ingredients in a heavy casserole and bake for about two hours.

Charcoal-Grilled Steak

As with charcoal-grilled lamb chops, steak for outdoor grilling is best cut thick, so that there is enough time for it to develop a good outside crust to contrast with a rare, juicy center. It's often convenient to have two steaks rather than one large one; this way, one can be cooked rare and the other medium.

1. Many different cuts of steak are excellent for outdoor grilling. Our favorite, however, is shell steak cut about 2" thick. It seems that this particular cut is called by a variety of names; it comes from the first cut of the short loin and essentially is a T-bone or porterhouse steak without the filet. A 2" shell steak will serve two people. (When buying steak allow ¾ to 1 pound for each serving.)

2. Use hardwood charcoal for grilling, and light the fire about a half hour before cooking the steaks.

3. Trim off any extra fat from the meat to prevent excessive flaring up of the fire, which would over-char the steak.

4. As mentioned in the recipe for charcoal-grilled lamb chops, there are a number of variables in outdoor cooking that make it difficult to give more than a rough estimate of cooking time. However, in general, a 2" steak will take 20 to 30 minutes to cook rare, and from 25 to 35 minutes to cook to a medium stage.

5. When the steak is done, grind over it black pepper and rock salt and place it on a hardwood cutting board or a hot platter. Cut away the bone with a sharp knife and carve the steak in diagonal slices.

Sauce Béarnaise

This is a smooth, light-textured, cooked butter sauce, distinctive for its pungent flavor of fresh tarragon and chervil. The herbs are essential to the sauce.

- 2 tablespoons finely chopped shallots
- ⅓ cup dry white wine
- ¼ cup tarragon vinegar
- 3 tablespoons finely cut tarragon leaves and stems plus 1 tablespoon finely cut tarragon leaves
- 2 tablespoons chervil leaves and stems plus 1 tablespoon finely cut chervil leaves
- ¼ teaspoon ground white pepper
- 1 stick butter
- 3 egg yolks
- ¼ teaspoon cayenne pepper
- ½ teaspoon salt (or to taste)

1. Place a small bowl and a fine sieve in a warm spot for use in the final step of preparing the sauce.

2. Place the shallots, wine, vinegar, salt and pepper in the top pan of a double boiler (Pyrex if you have one). Add the 3 tablespoons of tarragon and the 2 tablespoons of chervil, reserving a tablespoon of each to add to the sauce at the end.

3. Set the pan over medium heat and bring the mixture to a simmer. Continue to simmer until the liquid has reduced to 1 or 2 tablespoons. Set aside to cool slightly.

4. Heat water in the lower half of the double boiler until it is very hot, but not boiling.

5. Cut the butter into small pieces, and place the yolks close at hand.

6. As soon as the reduced liquid is just cool, place the pan over the hot water. Keep a low heat under the double boiler.

7. Spoon in one of the egg yolks, stirring briskly with a wire whisk. Add a few pieces of the butter and beat until smooth. Continue alternately adding the eggs and butter in this way.

8. Watch carefully that the water in the bottom of the double boiler doesn't boil, or the sauce may curdle (a Pyrex double boiler makes this step very easy).

9. As soon as the sauce reaches the consistency of a soft custard, set the pan into a container of cold water to prevent further cooking.

10. Press the sauce through the fine sieve into the warm bowl. Fold in the reserved tarragon and chervil and the cayenne pepper. Spoon the sauce into a serving bowl or sauce boat and serve at room temperature.

Braised Leeks

- 8 leeks
- 2 to 3 cups chicken broth
- Salt and freshly ground pepper to taste

1. Cut the leeks just below their green tops. Wash them well to remove any sand that may be lodged in the stalks.

2. Place the leeks in a casserole and add just enough broth to cover them. Cover the casserole loosely and cook about an hour in a preheated 350°F oven, or until the leeks are slightly transparent and tender to the prick of a wire cake tester or skewer.

3. Season with salt and freshly ground pepper.

NOTE: Braised leeks are delicious served either hot or cold.

Fresh Peach Cobbler with Nutmeg Sauce

Pie Crust

- 2 cups all-purpose flour
- ⅛ teaspoon salt
- 1½ sticks butter (6 ounces)
- ⅓ cup cold water

1. Prepare the pie dough and roll out the bottom crust as described in the recipe for deep-dish blackberry pie (page 33).

2. Sprinkle 2 tablespoons from the cup of sugar over the dough in an 8" x 8" x 2" Pyrex pie dish, and place the pie dish in the refrigerator until you are ready to put in the filling.

3. Traditionally, in Virginia, we always make a lattice top rather than a regular top crust for peach cobbler. To do this, roll out the remaining pie dough as usual and cut it into 8 strips.

Filling

- 7 large peaches
- 1 cup sugar
- ½ stick butter

1. About an hour and a half before you plan to serve the cobbler, remove the pie dish and lattice strips from the refrigerator. Preheat the oven to 450°F. Peel and slice the peaches. Sprinkle in half the remaining sugar over the bottom crust and add the sliced peaches, placing the last few slices in a mound in the center. Add the remaining sugar, and dot the peaches with about 8 or 9 thin pats of butter.

2. Weave 4 of the strips across the pie and 4 lengthwise. Moisten the rim with cold water and press down the lattice edges to seal them.

3. Set the cobbler on the middle rack of a 450°F oven for 10 minutes, then lower the heat to 425°F and bake for another 35 minutes.

4. Let the cobbler cool for a half hour and serve warm with nutmeg sauce.

Nutmeg Sauce

- ⅔ cup granulated sugar
- Pinch of salt
- 2 teaspoons cornstarch
- ¼ teaspoon freshly grated nutmeg
- 1 cup boiling water
- 1 2" piece dried orange peel
- 3 tablespoons brandy

1. Mix the sugar, salt, cornstarch, and nutmeg in a saucepan. Pour in the boiling water.

2. Place the saucepan over medium heat and add the orange peel. Let the sauce boil gently for 12 minutes. Longer cooking than this will change the flavor.

3. Remove the sauce from the burner and add the brandy. Cover the saucepan loosely and set aside until needed. When ready to serve, reheat without boiling and remove the orange peel.

NOTE: To make your own supply of dried orange peel, take 3 oranges and peel the rind without any of the pith. Place the rind on a rack to dry for 1 or 2 days. Store in a tight container and use as needed.

I like to use organically grown oranges for this. They're expensive but worth it. Health food shops carry them.

Edna Lewis with Jenny Fitch, co-owner of The Fearrington House Restaurant in Pittsboro, North Carolina. Edna served as guest chef here from 1983 to 1984.

Autumn & Winter
Dinner Menus

Coquilles St. Jacques (p. 59)
Roast Pheasant Stuffed with Wild Rice and White Grapes (p. 60)
Braised Celery (p. 61)
Compote of Lingonberries (p. 62)
French Bread
Romaine Lettuce Salad with French Dressing (p. 12)
Assorted Cheeses
Chestnut Cake (p. 62)
Coffee

Cold Poached Shrimp (p. 64)
Roast Capon (p. 64)
White Rice (p. 24)
French-Cut Green Beans with Parsley (p. 18)
Compote of Cranberries (p. 65)
Salad of Endive and Boston Lettuce with French Dressing (p. 12)
Assorted Cheeses
French Bread
Tart of Autumn Fruits (p. 66)
Coffee

Rib Pork Chops Sautéed (p. 67)
Whipped Sweet or White Potatoes (p. 68)
Boston Lettuce with French Dressing (p. 12)
Hot Buttered Rolls
Apple Brown Betty with Custard Sauce (p. 69)
Coffee

Thin Slices of Cranshaw Melon with Prosciutto (p. 31)
Lobster à l'Américain with White Rice (p. 70)
Hot Buttered French Bread
Bibb Lettuce with French Dressing (p. 12)
Chocolate Soufflé with Whipped Cream and Chocolate Sauce (p. 72)
Coffee

Oysters on the Half Shell Broiled with Buttered Bread Crumbs (p. 74)
Roast Ribs of Pork with Peanut Sauce (p. 75)
Sautéed Paper-Thin White Potatoes (p. 76)
French-Cut Green Beans (p. 18)
Mixed Green Salad
Deep-Dish Apple Pie with Nutmeg Sauce (p. 77)
Coffee

Lobster Cocktail with Special Sauce (p. 9)
Crisp Roast Duck Garnished with Kumquats (p. 78)
Wild Rice (p. 17)
Green Beans (p. 18)
Boston Lettuce with French Dressing (p. 12)
French Bread
Assorted Cheeses
Soufflé Grand Marnier with Orange Sauce (p. 80)
Coffee

Sautéed Scallops with a Ring of White Rice (p. 81)
Salad of Mixed Greens
French Bread
Cheeses
Individual Chocolate Soufflé with
Chocolate Sauce and Whipped Cream (p. 72)
Coffee

Beef with Onions and Red Wine (p. 82)
Freshly-Made Noodles (p. 83)
Romaine Lettuce Salad
Hot-Buttered French Bread
Assorted Cheeses
Apricot Custard Tart (p. 84)
Coffee

❧

Melon Slices with Prosciutto (p. 31)
Roast Veal Garnished with Carrots and Sautéed Mushrooms (p. 85)
Sautéed Potato Balls (p. 12)
Romaine Lettuce with Italian Watercress
French Bread
Crêpes Suzette (p. 86)
Coffee

Coquilles St. Jacques

Scallops

- 1 pound bay scallops
- 3 tablespoons butter
- 3 tablespoons finely chopped shallots
- 2 teaspoons flour
- 3 tablespoons dry sherry
- ¾ cup heavy cream
- Salt to taste
- Pinch of cayenne pepper
- 2 sprigs parsley

1. Preheat the oven to 425°F.
2. Place the scallops in a 10" skillet and bring gently to a medium heat. The scallops will give off liquid as they cook. Shake the pan constantly and stir carefully, using a wooden spoon to avoid cutting these very tender shellfish. Watch carefully that they do not boil in their liquid as this tends to toughen them.
3. Cook the scallops only until they are heated through. This will take about 5 minutes. Then turn them into a casserole and start your sauce.
4. To prepare the sauce, bring the 3 tablespoons of butter to the foaming stage, add the chopped shallots, and sauté without browning for about 5 minutes. Blend in the flour and cook for another few minutes.
5. With a perforated spoon, lift the scallops from the casserole and place them in a bowl. Strain the liquid from the casserole into the shallot mixture, and stir and simmer for 3 or 4 minutes. Add the sherry and continue to let it simmer a few minutes longer.
6. Bring the cream to a hard boil in a wide saucepan or skillet until it has reduced by half. Stir the reduced cream into the sauce and season with salt and cayenne pepper. Mix well and strain into a bowl containing the scallops. There should be ample sauce to cover the scallops, but if it seems scant, add more hot cream and correct the seasoning. Cover the bowl and set it in a warm place.

Crumb Topping

- ½ cup freshly made bread crumbs
- 2 teaspoons melted butter
- 2 teaspoons chopped parsley
- Pinch finely chopped garlic (optional)

1. Butter lightly and fill four scallop shells or ramekins with the scallop mixture. Mix the bread crumbs with the melted butter and sprinkle them evenly over the shells.
2. Place the shells in the oven about 12 minutes until the surfaces are brown and bubbling. Remove, sprinkle over the parsley, and serve.

NOTE: The bubbling indicates that the scallops are succulent and at their peak; if they remain in the oven past this stage, they will dry out and the special qualities of this dish will be lost.

Because scallops are very sweet and delicate in flavor, I refrain from seasoning them too highly, as it would destroy their natural sweetness.

Roast Pheasant Stuffed with Wild Rice and White Grapes

To my taste pheasant are more flavorful and better textured, as well as meatier, than chickens and deserve to be more popular. While many people seem to think of pheasant, quail, and partridge as sophisticated fare, it has been my experience that people living in the country are far more familiar with the special and delicious taste of game birds than are most city dwellers.

Pheasant, whether wild or domestic, have very little taste—in fact practically none—if they are killed, dressed, and cooked right away. They seem to reach their peak of flavor when they are hung, still feathered, in a cold place for at least a week. Some butchers will do this if requested and will also pluck them after the birds have aged.

Pheasant have more white meat than chicken, and it remains deliciously moist and tender if served cold the following day, so you may wish to roast one more than you will need for dinner.

- 1 pheasant (allow 1 for 2 people)
- 1 stick plus 1 tablespoon butter
- 1 teaspoon salt
- ½ teaspoon pepper
- ¼ teaspoon thyme
- Watercress garnish
- 1½ cups cooked wild rice
- ⅓ cup seedless white (green) grapes

1. Carefully wash and pat dry the outside of the pheasant. Remove the lungs and entrails from the inside cavity and wipe it well with a damp cloth. Do not wash out the cavity, as it will take away some of the special flavor that is characteristic of game birds.

2. Mix together the salt, pepper, and thyme. If the thyme is fresh, cut it fine; if dry, crush it against the salt with a spoon.

3. Sprinkle the cavity with half this mixture and add ½ stick of butter.

4. Rub the outside with 1 to 2 tablespoons of soft butter and the rest of the seasoning.

5. Stuff the cavity with hot cooked wild rice (see page 17 for wild rice recipe).

6. Roast in a covered casserole or roasting pan in the middle of a 425°F oven. Allow 1½ hours for cooking. After 15 minutes lower the heat to 350°F. Melt the remaining ½ stick of butter, and after reducing the heat, baste every quarter

hour with a tablespoon of melted butter.

7. Twenty minutes before the pheasant is done, place the grapes in the cavity with the wild rice. At this point you may find it convenient to transfer the bird to another casserole to finish cooking so that you can make the sauce, which is easily done.

8. Add 3 tablespoons of hot water to the juices in the first casserole and stir well to loosen any particles stuck to the bottom. Strain and reheat just before serving.

9. Remove the pheasant from the oven and place it on a hot serving dish with a garnish of watercress.

Braised Celery

- **2 bunches celery**
- **1 tablespoon salt**
- **2½ to 3 cups beef broth**
- **4 to 6 thin pats butter**
- **Finely cut parsley**

1. Wash and trim celery. Pull off any coarse outside fibers and cut the celery into 5" lengths.

2. Plunge the celery into a pot of boiling water, add the salt, and parboil for 15 minutes. Remove the celery, drain, and place in a casserole.

3. Pour in just enough beef broth to come to the top of the celery without covering it. Dot with thin pats of butter, cover the casserole, and set in a 350°F oven to braise for about 45 minutes.

4. Quarter the celery lengthwise before serving and sprinkle with the parsley.

Compote of Lingonberries

Lingonberries are small mountain cranberries. We find them a pleasant change from cranberries as they are lighter in texture and tangier in taste.

Unfortunately, they are not widely available, but the best places to seek them out are in Scandinavian grocery stores or in delicacy shops and the best time is during the autumn and winter months. They are sold from the barrel, and since they keep well, buy 2 or 3 quarts at a time and then stew them as needed.

- **1 pint lingonberries**
- **3 to 4 tablespoons sugar**

1. To prepare a pint, first pick over the berries, removing any leaves, bits of stem, or bruised berries. Cook them in the juice that has collected at the bottom of the container they have been stored in, adding 3 or 4 tablespoons of sugar. Bring to a full foaming boil and remove them from the burner. Serve them warm or cold as you would cranberries.

Chestnut Cake

Because fresh chestnuts are available only in late fall until about Christmas time, this cake is a very special seasonal treat.

Cake

- **2 pounds fresh chestnuts**
- **2 cups grated boiled chestnuts**
- **1½ sticks butter**
- **1 cup sugar**
- **4 eggs, separated**
- **2 tablespoons rum**

1. Remove the eggs and butter from the refrigerator so that they will be at room temperature when you begin to mix the cake batter.

2. Next prepare the chestnuts. You will need 2 pounds of nuts to make 2 cups of grated chestnuts.

3. Score the flat side of the chestnuts with the point of a sharp knife to break the skin.

4. Place the nuts in a saucepan and cover with boiling water. Simmer for about an hour. To make certain they are done, peel one of the chestnuts and slice it in half. It should be dry and mealy and resemble a baked potato in texture.

5. Cool the nuts in the water until you can handle them easily, then peel. Don't let them become cold, or they will be really difficult to peel.

6. Put them through a food mill or a nut grater. To avoid packing down, use a light touch with your spoon when measuring the grated nuts.

7. Preheat the oven to 350°F.

8. Cream the butter with the back of a spoon until it is satiny (if you are using an electric mixer, beat at medium-low speed). Add the sugar gradually until it is well blended with the butter and the texture is light and fluffy.

9. Beat the egg yolks in a separate bowl, then add and mix them in well.

10. Add the rum. Stir in the grated chestnuts and mix until they are thoroughly blended.

11. Beat the egg whites until they are stiff, but not dry. Gently fold them into the cake batter. Be careful not to overmix or you will risk breaking down the egg whites.

12. Spoon the mixture into 2 8" layer-cake pans with removable bottoms.

13. Bake for 25 minutes.

14. Remove the cakes from the oven. After a few minutes, slide a thin knife around the edge of the cakes and slip off the rims. This is a rather fragile cake, so don't attempt to remove the cake-pan bottoms until the cakes are cold. Set the layers on racks to cool.

Glaze

- **1 square unsweetened chocolate**
- **2 tablespoons butter**

1. When the cakes have cooled, make the chocolate glaze. Place the chocolate and butter in a small pan over hot water. Stir until the chocolate has melted and the mixture is smooth. Keep it warm while you whip the cream.

Filling

- **⅔ cup heavy cream, whipped, sweetened to taste, and flavored with vanilla**

1. Whip cream until thickened, sweeten to taste, and flavor with vanilla, mixing lightly. Spread one layer of the cake with the whipped cream, cover with the second layer, and dribble the chocolate glaze over the top and sides of the cake.

Cold Poached Shrimp

- **1½ pounds shrimp**
- **Bouillon for poaching (see page 9)**

1. Bring the bouillon to a boil and drop in the shrimp. Cover and wait until the bouillon returns to a boil, then immediately lower the heat to a simmer and cook for 6 minutes.

2. Remove the pan from the burner and place on a rack. Uncover and let the shrimp cool for about an hour in the broth.

3. Remove the shells, devein the shrimp, and refrigerate in a bowl covered tightly with wax paper. When you are ready to serve the shrimp arrange them on beds of crisp lettuce and serve with special sauce (see page 9).

Roast Capon

The two essential elements in making a perfect roast capon or chicken are roasting at high temperature and serving immediately upon removing it from the oven. Then the deliciously crisp skin obtained from the high heat will not have time to collapse and become soft.

- **5-to-6-pound capon**
- **1 stick plus 2 tablespoons butter**
- **Salt**
- **Pepper**
- **Garnish of watercress**

1. Preheat the oven to 450°F.

2. Wash the capon under cold running water and dry well. Rub the cavity with salt and pepper and a half stick of butter. Tie or fasten the legs together, and smooth 1 to 2 tablespoons of soft butter over the outside of the capon.

3. I allow an hour and a half for roasting. This seems to be perfect timing, even though there is some slight variation in the weight of the bird. Plan carefully so that the end of the hour and a half will coincide with the time you plan to serve the main course.

4. Place the capon in a shallow roasting pan and set it in the middle rack of the preheated oven. Melt a half stick of butter. After the capon has roasted for 45 minutes, baste with a tablespoonful of melted butter every 15 minutes. While basting watch for the point at which the juices from the chicken drain out and form a thick and syrupy consistency in the pan. When this begins to happen, pour the juices into a small bowl or

saucepan. If they cook beyond this point, the liquid will evaporate, and only an oily residue will remain.

5. Remove the bird from the oven and place it on a heated platter. Set it back in the oven or in a warm place while you prepare the sauce. Add a tablespoon of hot water to the roasting pan and stir and strain the pan drippings into a saucepan with the juices that were poured off earlier. Heat without boiling, season, and serve with the roast.

6. Place watercress around the capon before serving.

Compote of Cranberries

- 1 quart cranberries
- 1 cup granulated sugar
- 1¼ cups water
- Almond oil
- Chicory

1. Wash and pick over the berries and discard any bruised ones, pieces of stem, or leaves.

2. Place the cranberries in a saucepan with the sugar and water and bring them to a boil. The skins will start to pop open, and after most of the berries have popped, boil them another 3 to 4 minutes.

3. Remove the cranberries from the burner and let them cool, then press them through a sieve to remove the seeds and skins. Pour the strained berries into a decorative mold that has been brushed with almond oil (or water), and set in the refrigerator to chill. Serve on a bed of chicory.

Tart of Autumn Fruits

⌒⸺⌒

This is a dessert beautiful to see as well as delightful to taste in its blend of flavors and textures. Preheat the oven to 400°F, then prepare the pastry and bake the tart shell (see page 21). The fruits for this tart are baked separately. When both the pastry and the fruits have cooled, fill the tart and glaze with the reduced fruit juices.

If you oven-cook the fruits instead of poaching them, they will keep a better shape, and—important to the flavor of this tart—the juices from the fruits will blend together to make a delicious syrup for glazing the tart.

- **2 pounds fresh purple plums**
- **2 pounds fresh peaches**
- **1 pound fresh apricots (or ¼ pound dried apricots)**
- **⅔ cup granulated sugar**
- **1 9" baked tart shell (page 21)**

1. Use dried apricots if fresh ones are not available, and follow the directions for cooking given in the apricot custard tart on page 84. Substitute frozen peaches if you cannot find fresh ones, but bake them for only half the time suggested for fresh peaches.

2. Because peaches take longer to cook than other fruits, prepare them first. Peel them, slice in eighths, and arrange the slices so that they slightly overlap in one section of a baking dish large enough to hold all the fruits. Sprinkle with 3 tablespoons of the sugar and place the dish in the middle rack of the oven for 15 minutes.

3. While the peaches are baking, prepare the plums and apricots by cutting them in halves and removing the pits.

4. Remove the baking dish with the peaches. Arrange the plums with the cut side up in one part of the dish, and the apricots, cut side down, in another. Sprinkle over the remaining sugar and return the dish to the oven. Bake the fruits another 15 minutes, basting 2 or 3 times with the juices.

5. When all the fruits seem tender (if a toothpick pierces the fruit easily without any resistance, it has baked long enough), remove the casserole from the oven and spoon off the syrup into a small saucepan. As the fruits cool, spoon off any more juices that appear.

6. Place the saucepan over medium heat and bring the syrup to a boil. Let it continue to boil rapidly for about 4 minutes, until it thickens. Be careful not to overcook the syrup or you will destroy its delicate flavor. Set aside to cool.

7. When the syrup has cooled, coat the bottom of the tart crust, brushing the syrup on with a pastry brush or smoothing it with the back of a spoon.

8. Arrange the fruits in the tart shell with the plums cut side up and the apricots cut side down, the same way as for baking. Begin with an outer circle of plums, then make a circle of overlapping

peach slices. Continue with 2 circles of the plums, 2 of peaches, and 1 of apricots. Place an apricot in the center of the tart; or, if you like, fill the center with fresh raspberries.

9. Glaze the fruit by spooning over the remaining syrup.

10. Serve the tart at room temperature with a bowl of vanilla-flavored sweetened whipped cream.

Rib Pork Chops Sautéed

- **Rib pork chops for 4**
- **½ cup all-purpose flour**
- **½ cup whole-wheat flour**
- **1 teaspoon freshly ground pepper**
- **1½ teaspoons salt**
- **2 tablespoons butter or lard**
- **Garnish of watercress**

1. Order rib chops half an inch thick and sliced from the center cut. Ask the butcher to bone each chop and to bind each one with a strip of fat cut from the loin and secured with a string or small skewer.

2. Mix well the flour and seasonings and spread the mixture out on a platter or on a sheet of wax paper.

3. Press the chops in the flour and set them aside for about an hour before you cook them.

4. If you use lard for your frying fat, heat the lard in the skillet until it sizzles when a drop of water is flicked in and then add the chops. If you use butter, heat the skillet over medium heat, add the butter, and when the foaming begins to subside and the butter begins to brown at the edges of the pan, add the chops.

5. Cook covered throughout. The first side should cook to a rich brown in 12 minutes. Turn the chops, lower the flame to medium-low, and cook another 12 to 15 minutes.

6. Remove the chops to a heated platter. Tilt the pan so that you can dip off about half the fat. Return the pan to the burner over high heat and pour in ¼ cup of water. Boil hard until the sauce reaches a syrupy consistency, then pour it over the chops. Garnish the chops with watercress.

Whipped White Potatoes

- **5 to 6 medium-sized Idaho potatoes**
- **½ stick butter**
- **1 cup hot milk**
- **2 teaspoons salt**
- **½ teaspoon freshly ground white pepper**
- **2 teaspoons freshly cut parsley or some finely cut chives**

1. Wash and pare the potatoes. Place them in a saucepan and pour in boiling water to cover. Add the salt and cook briskly for 20 minutes.

2. Drain and mash with a potato masher or put them through a Foley mill. Add the butter, pepper, and salt to taste.

3. Pour in the hot milk and mix well by hand or with an electric mixer until the potatoes are light and fluffy.

4. Spoon the mixture into a heated casserole, dot with butter, and set under the broiler to slightly brown the peaks.

5. Sprinkle over with the parsley or chives and serve piping hot.

Whipped Sweet Potatoes

- **4 medium-sized sweet potatoes or yams**
- **1 stick soft butter**
- **⅓ cup brandy**
- **2 tablespoons brown sugar**
- **Fresh grated nutmeg**

1. Place the potatoes in a saucepan and pour in boiling water to cover. Cook for 30 minutes or until the potatoes are cooked through.

2. Drain, peel, and put the potatoes through a food mill or sieve.

3. Add the soft butter and brandy and whip the potatoes by hand or with an electric beater.

4. When the mixture is light and smooth, spoon in up to the top of a heated casserole. Don't even off the top, but leave in a free-form shape.

5. Sprinkle over with the brown sugar and a grating of fresh nutmeg. Set into a hot oven until the potatoes are well heated. Serve hot.

Apple Brown Betty
with Custard Sauce

W e did a number of tests on the apply betty with various types of bread and different kinds of apples. Our final choices were dried French bread and McIntosh apples. While McIntosh apples seemed to have a tendency to cook up rather rapidly into applesauce if not watched carefully toward the end of the baking period, we decided in favor of them as they have good flavor, are juicy, and are the most widely and easily available.

We started out by using 1 stick of butter, but found it was too rich after the pork. The reduction to 2 tablespoons actually seemed to make a lighter, happier betty!

We began to test this recipe in September and used no water. However, by early winter, as the apples became drier, we found it necessary to add water or the apples were likely to remain hard and dry even after an hour of baking.

Apple Brown Betty

- **5 large McIntosh apples (2 pounds)**
- **½ cup sugar**
- **1½ teaspoons freshly grated nutmeg**
- **3 cups ¼" cubes bread**
- **2 tablespoons melted butter**
- **Grated lemon rind**
- **2 to 4 tablespoons cold water**

1. French bread that is one or two days old makes very good crumbs. If you are using packaged white bread, remove 5 to 6 slices early in the day to dry; or place them for 10 to 15 minutes in a slow oven until they are dry but not brown. Cut the bread into small cubes.

2. Grate the nutmeg and mix with the sugar. Melt the butter and sprinkle it over the diced bread, toss, and stir in all but 2 tablespoons of the sugar mixture. Grate over the lemon rind and mix well.

3. Line the bottom of a heavy 1½ quart baking dish with a cup of the breadcrumb mixture.

4. Peel, quarter and core the apples.

5. Arrange half the sliced apples in the casserole. Cover with ½ cup of the bread cubes. Add the remaining apple slices and sprinkle with the water. Top with the rest of the bread and sprinkle the 2 tablespoons of reserved sugar over the top.

6. Cover tightly (if your baking dish doesn't have a lid, use foil), and place the betty in the center of a preheated oven at 375°F. Uncover after 40 minutes and bake 10 to 15 minutes longer or until the apples are tender and the top is brown. Serve warm (if cooked too far in advance of the meal, the brown betty will fall) with vanilla-flavored custard sauce.

Custard Sauce

We tried several different combinations of whole eggs, yolks, varying amounts of milk and cream and then agreed that this is the best for making a custard sauce that is not too rich and yet of a good consistency.

- 2 cups milk
- 3 egg yolks
- 1 whole egg
- ⅓ cup sugar
- ½ vanilla bean
- 1 teaspoon vanilla extract

1. Scald the milk with the vanilla bean. Slightly beat the eggs, then beat the sugar into the eggs until they are well mixed and light.
2. Remove the vanilla bean and slowly stir in the scalded milk.
3. Pour the mixture into a heavy-bottomed saucepan and place over low heat. Stir constantly until the spoon has a heavy coat (about 8 minutes), then immediately place the saucepan into a pan of cold water. Stir the custard rapidly to quickly cool it and to keep it from further cooking.
4. Strain the sauce through a fine sieve. Cool, and when well chilled flavor with vanilla extract.

Lobster à l'Américain

Lobster à l'Américain is a treat any time of the year, but it is especially memorable when made at the end of summer or in early fall when fresh tomatoes and herbs are available. Basically, it consists of a tomato sauce, which can be made a day in advance, and pan-broiled lobster. The two are combined and enriched in flavor and texture with the addition of brandy and cream.

Lobsters

- 4 live and active lobsters, 1¼ to 1½ pounds each
- ½ cup brandy

Cooking the Lobsters

1. About 40 minutes before serving, wash the lobsters under cold running water to remove any grit or seaweed. Grasp them from the back at the point where the tail joins the body. Set them to drain in a large pan.
2. Heat a large, heavy-bottomed skillet until it is sizzling hot. While the pan is heating, clip off the lobster legs with kitchen or poultry shears. (You can freeze the legs and use them later for a lobster sauce or bisque.)
3. As soon as the skillet is hot, put in the lobsters. Pour in ½ cup of the brandy

and flame it. Cover the skillet and cook the lobsters over low heat for 20 minutes. Remove the skillet from the heat and uncover.

4. Lift out the lobsters one at a time and, holding them over a large bowl, cut them up with poultry shears. Discard the heads and midsections. Cut each tail into 3 pieces and crack the claws.

Sauce

- ⅛ **pound bacon cubed (or 3 to 4 slices of bacon cut up)**
- ½ **stick butter**
- **2 medium onions**
- **1 bunch scallions**
- **2 cups peeled and seeded fresh tomatoes or 2 cups tomato purée**
- **1 bay leaf**
- ¼ **teaspoon fresh or dried thyme**

1. Render the bacon in a medium-sized, heavy-bottomed skillet over medium heat.

2. While the bacon is cooking, finely chop the scallions and onions.

3. Remove the defatted pieces of bacon from the skillet, add the butter, then when it is hot add the scallions and onions. Sauté until they are soft but not brown and add the tomatoes (or tomato purée), bay leaf, and thyme. Let simmer for 45 minutes.

Final Steps

- ⅓ **cup brandy**
- **Pinch cayenne pepper**
- **Salt to taste**
- ⅓ **cup heavy cream**
- **2 teaspoons finely cut parsley**
- **2 teaspoons fresh tarragon (if available)**

1. Empty into a large skillet the bowl of tail pieces, claws, and liquid that drained out while you cut up the lobsters.

2. Pour in the tomato sauce. Add ⅓ cup brandy and the cayenne pepper and simmer for 10 minutes. Salt to taste.

3. Stir in the cream and heat through without allowing the sauce to boil. Add the finely cut parsley and fresh tarragon. Serve with a large bowl of fluffy white rice.

Chocolate Soufflé with Whipped Cream and Chocolate Sauce

The first chocolate soufflé I made at Café Nicholson was so warmly accepted by the few customers who sampled it that I began to make them every day. They became so popular that in the end they were the only dessert we served except "pear and cheese."

At that time I was unaware of all the supposed pitfalls of soufflé making. I baked them in small soup bowls. I never measured ingredients, but each day shortly before the dinner hour I made about a pint of roux and added a lot of grated bitter chocolate. I used less yolks than whites because I found this made a lighter and less yolky-tasting batter.

My real guide in making them was the comments from the guests, such as "It's so light," "So full of chocolate," and "Not too sweet." And they loved the addition I thought up one day of serving the soufflés with a light, slightly bitter chocolate sauce and a heaping bowl of whipped cream.

I had no set time for cooking them. Our waitress developed a fine sense of timing with experience, and she would tell me when it was time to set the soufflés in the oven for each table.

We had only one oven. Orders were coming in at different times, so the oven door was constantly being opened and closed! Sometimes the soufflés would have to be carried 150 feet away to the rear of the garden. Yet we never had a problem of fallen soufflés.

One evening a soufflé was overlooked in the oven. When I removed it, it just collapsed. It was then that it came to me that as long as there was moisture in a soufflé it would continue to rise. Without realizing it, I had been removing the soufflés from the oven before they were fully baked. The heat from the batter that was still soft and moist plus the heat of the bowl allowed them to continue cooking as they were being carried to the tables! The result was that they were presented to the diners at their full height, and as Clementine Paddleford in her column in the *New York Herald Tribune* described them, as ". . . light as a dandelion seed in a high wind."

Chocolate Soufflé

- 4 ounces bitter chocolate, grated
- 2 tablespoons butter
- 2 tablespoons flour
- ¼ teaspoon salt
- 1 cup milk, scalded
- ½ vanilla bean
- 3 tablespoons sugar
- 3 egg yolks
- 5 egg whites

1. Grate the 4 squares of chocolate on the next to the finest side of a 4-sided grater.

2. Melt the butter in a heavy saucepan over medium heat. Add the flour and cook a few minutes without browning until the flour is well blended. Remove the saucepan from the heat.

3. Scald the milk with the vanilla bean. Remove the bean and add the hot milk to the butter-flour mixture, stirring rapidly until the mixture is thick and smooth. Add the grated chocolate, which will melt when it is stirred in.

4. Continue stirring and add ⅓ cup of hot water. Next add 3 lightly beaten egg yolks, salt, and 3 tablespoons of sugar.

5. Stir the batter vigorously for about 4 or 5 minutes, until it appears smooth and satiny. This part of the preparation can be done a half hour or so ahead of time. Just be sure to cover the saucepan lightly with waxed paper and place in a warm spot until you are ready to whip the egg whites and cook the soufflé.

6. Preheat the oven to 450°F.

7. Whip the whites to soft peaks. Stir the chocolate mixture well and fold in the whipped egg whites. Fold in thoroughly, but lightly, with a large flat spoon or rubber spatula, cutting down through the mixture and bringing the spoon up and over with a folding motion.

8. Spoon the batter into one 2-quart soufflé dish or four to six individual dishes approximately three-fourths full. Make sure the soufflé dishes are hot, as this helps hasten cooking.

9. Set the dishes in the oven and raise the heat to 475°F for 5 minutes to make up for the heat loss that takes place when the dishes are set in, then lower it to 450°F.

10. Cook individual soufflés from 12 to 13 minutes. A single 2-quart dish will take from 20 to 25 minutes (a chocolate soufflé needs longer cooking time than other kinds of soufflés).

11. Remove from the oven. Dust the soufflés with powdered sugar and serve with hot chocolate sauce and whipped cream.

Chocolate Sauce

- 1½ ounces bitter chocolate
- 1 cup water
- 2 tablespoons sugar
- Small piece vanilla bean

1. To make the sauce, grate the chocolate and place in a saucepan with the water, sugar, and vanilla bean. Bring to a boil and let simmer 15 to 20 minutes. Remove from the burner and set aside until needed.

NOTE: This sauce can be made ahead and reheated before serving.

Whipped Cream

- 1 cup heavy cream
- 1 to 2 tablespoons sugar
- 2 teaspoons vanilla extract

1. Whip the cream just until it holds its own shape, sweeten to taste, and flavor with the vanilla extract.

Oysters on the Half Shell Broiled with Buttered Bread Crumbs

- 12 or 16 oysters
- ½ cup fine bread crumbs seasoned with 1 teaspoon paprika
- 1 stick butter, melted

1. Place the oysters in the deeper side of their shells and arrange them in a shallow pan lined with either rock salt or crumpled aluminum foil to keep them in place.

2. Set the pan about 3 inches under a preheated broiler for about 5 minutes until the edges of the oysters begin to ruffle, or curl.

3. Remove the pan and sprinkle 1 teaspoon of bread crumbs and a generous teaspoon of butter over each oyster. Return to the broiler for another 5 minutes until the oysters are bubbling and golden in color.

4. Place them on four individual serving dishes, garnish with lemon wedges and parsley, and serve while still bubbling.

Roast Ribs of Pork with Peanut Sauce

I have found that roast ribs of pork are both juicier and more flavorful than the tenderloin. Also, the ribs serve as a good case to hold the meat together while it roasts.

Roast Ribs of Pork

- 5 to 6 pounds loin of pork cut from the rib end (about 12 chops)
- 2 teaspoons salt
- 1 teaspoon freshly ground pepper
- ¼ teaspoon powdered ginger
- Watercress, enough to cover serving platter

1. Preheat the oven at 400°F for 15 minutes.
2. Carve the meat out of the ribs in one whole piece. Mix together the salt, pepper, and ginger and rub it into the meat. Place it back against the ribs, and tie in place with white string in about 4 places.
3. Place the roast fat side up on a double sheet of greased foil. Draw the foil close to the meat to form a 1½" to 2" deep trough that will hold the juices close to the meat. This will help keep the pork juicy inside and crisp outside.
4. Set the roast in a shallow baking pan, and place in the center of the oven. Allow 2 to 2½ hours for roasting.
5. Baste the pork 4 or 5 times with the pan juices.
6. When the pork has turned a rich brown and is springy to the touch, and the juices run clear when you prick it with a fork, remove it from the oven. Lift the meat off the foil and place it on a heated platter. Set it back in the oven or in a warm place while you prepare the sauce.
7. To make the sauce, you will want the juices that collected in the foil. Pour them into a bowl or saucepan and skim off the fat before adding them to the peanut mixture.
8. Just before serving, cut the strings tied around the roast, then lift the meat off the ribs and place on a bed of watercress on a warm serving platter.

Peanut Sauce

- ¼ clove garlic
- ¼ teaspoon cayenne or sambal oclek*
- ¼ cup peanut butter
- ½ tablespoon vinegar
- ½ tablespoon soy sauce or ketjap benteng asin†
- 1 cup water
- Salt to taste

1. Heat a 9" skillet and add 2 tablespoons of fat from the roasting pork. Sauté the garlic and cayenne without browning. Mix together the remaining ingredients and add them to the garlic mixture. Stir

---

* A Southeast Asian chile sauce.
† A Southeast Asian soy sauce.

well, then set aside the sauce until the pork is done.

2. Add the defatted meat drippings, blend thoroughly with the peanut mixture, and taste for seasoning.

3. If the sauce seems too thick, add a bit of hot water.

4. Serve hot with the roast pork.

Sautéed Paper-Thin White Potatoes

- **4 Idaho potatoes (1½ pounds)**
- **⅔ stick butter**

1. About 20 minutes before you plan to serve dinner, peel the potatoes and slice them paper thin with a vegetable peeler or a sharp knife over a bowl or plate.

2. Heat a 12" skillet and add the butter. As soon as the butter reaches the foaming stage and begins to brown, add the potatoes.

3. Cover the pan so that the potatoes heat all the way through. After 4 minutes, remove the cover and turn the potatoes over with a wide spatula, as you would pancakes. The slices that have been on the bottom will have turned a bright golden brown; slide these over to the side of the pan. As more slices brown, keep moving them aside until all the potatoes are crisp and brown. This will take about 10 minutes altogether.

4. If the potatoes are ready a little before you have finished the other preparations, slide them into a pan lined with brown paper or paper toweling and put them in a warm oven.

Deep-Dish Apple Pie
with Nutmeg Sauce

Pie Crust

- 2 cups all-purpose flour
- ⅛ teaspoon salt
- 1½ sticks butter (6 ounces)
- ⅓ cup cold water

1. See the recipe for deep-dish blackberry pie on page 33 for detailed instructions in preparing the pie crust.

2. Allow 15 minutes to preheat the oven to 450°F.

3. Remove the dough from the refrigerator about 15 to 20 minutes before rolling it out, so that it will be soft and easy to handle. Roll out the bottom crust into a 10" square, then roll it onto the pin and carefully unroll it over an 8" x 8" x 2" Pyrex pie dish. Gently shape it into the bottom and sides of the dish.

Filling

- 7 large apples (about 3 pounds)— Cortland, McIntosh, or any tart apple of good flavor
- 1 teaspoon freshly grated nutmeg
- ⅔ cup sugar
- 5 thin pats chilled butter

1. Peel the apples, quarter, core, and seed them, and slice each quarter into 4 slices. Place the apple wedges in layers in the pan, and when half full, sprinkle with the nutmeg and half the sugar. Fill the pan with apples until they are level with the top, and then slice an additional apple, placing it in a mound in the center. Dot the apples with the pats of butter and add the remaining sugar.

2. Roll out the top crust and unroll it off the rolling pin over the apples. Firm it down gently with your fingers and trim off any edges.

3. Make vents all over the top crust with a pointed knife, but not closer than 2 inches from the edge, or the juices will run out and over the edge of the pan.

4. Place the pie in the middle rack of the preheated oven for 10 minutes, then lower the heat to 425°F and bake an additional 40 minutes.

5. Let cool for a half hour and serve with nutmeg sauce (page 51) and vanilla ice cream.

Crisp Roast Duck
Garnished with Kumquats

⌇⎯⎯⎯⎯⌇

Perhaps the most distinctive characteristic of a perfectly roasted duck is the marvelous contrast between the crisp, crackling skin and the succulent, tender meat. The most important steps in achieving this perfection are a long, thorough drying of the ducks and the orange or tangerine stuffing (which not only gives delicious flavor to the meat, but also keeps it juicy). High roasting temperature is also essential.

Roast Duck

- ✿ **2 5-pound ducks**
- ✿ **3 mandarin oranges, if available, or tangerines**
- ✿ **2 tablespoons soft butter**
- ✿ **2 teaspoons salt**
- ✿ **½ teaspoon pepper, freshly ground**

1. It is advisable to prepare your ducks the night before you plan to cook them, or early in the morning of the same day. When fresh ducks are not available, frozen ones can be used successfully but should be purchased a day ahead to allow time for thawing. Remove the wrapper before thawing. It will take about 12 hours for a frozen duck to thaw in the refrigerator or in a cool place. Don't thaw by soaking in warm water.

2. Wash the ducks inside and out and pat dry. Cut away any excess skin from the neck. Cut the wings off at the second joint, taking care not to tear any skin.

3. Remove the fat that clings to the opening or to the inside of the cavity.

4. Peel an orange, cut it in half, and rub it over the ducks.

5. Place the ducks on a rack so that the air can circulate around them, and dry the skin. It's amazing to see the skin turn paper-dry and almost transparent, like fine parchment, after several hours of drying.

6. Fifteen minutes before roasting, preheat the oven to 450°F.

7. Combine the salt and pepper with the butter. Rub the insides of the ducklings with the seasoned butter. Peel, quarter, and remove the seeds of two oranges and place them in the cavities. Close the bottom opening to the cavity with a skewer or by sewing the edges loosely together; do not let the skin overlap.

8. Set the ducks breast side up on an oiled rack that has been raised at least 2" from the bottom of the roasting pan so that the heat can pass over and under the birds. Set the pan on the middle rack of the oven. Allow two hours for cooking the ducks.

9. After 10 minutes lower the heat to 425°F.

10. Drain the fat from the ducks 3 or 4 times during the roasting period. Lift off the rack with the ducks and place it in a pan. Tilt the rack in order to pour out any juices that have collected in the cavities and reserve for the sauce. Drain the fat in the roasting pan into a separate container to discard when cool. Set the rack back in the pan and return the ducklings to the oven.

11. About 30 minutes before the ducks are finished roasting, prepare the sauce.

Sauce

- 4 tablespoons granulated sugar
- 4 tablespoons Grand Marnier
- 1 tablespoon red-wine or cider vinegar
- ½ cup orange juice
- 2 tablespoons butter
- 1 leek, finely chopped
- 1 carrot, grated
- ½ tablespoon flour
- Grated rind of 2 oranges
- 1 tablespoon brandy

1. To make the sauce, melt the sugar in a heavy-bottomed skillet over medium heat until it turns light amber. Remove the pan from the burner and pour in the Grand Marnier, vinegar, and orange juice. Stir well to dissolve the caramel. Set aside.

2. Melt the butter in another small frying pan and sauté the leek and carrot until soft, but do not brown. Add the flour and, stirring all the while, sauté another few minutes.

3. Pour the juices that were drained from the duck cavities into the pan with the caramel mixture. Add the sautéed vegetables and let the sauce simmer for 15 minutes. When the ducks are nearly ready, skim off the fat that has risen to the surface of the sauce. Add the grated rind of 2 oranges and season with the brandy and salt and pepper to taste. Reheat the sauce without boiling.

4. When the ducks are finished roasting, cut them in halves or quarters. Garnish with fresh poached kumquats and serve with the sauce.

Poached Kumquats

- 1 or 2 boxes kumquats
- 1½ cups sugar
- 2 cups water

1. Poach the kumquats by first making a syrup with the combined sugar and water.

2. Cut a few slits in each kumquat and gently cook them in the syrup until they are soft or for about a half hour. Drain to use as a garnish.

Soufflé Grand Marnier
with Orange Sauce

Soufflé

- 1 cup orange juice
- 6 tablespoons sugar
- 3 tablespoons butter
- 3 yolks from medium-sized eggs
- ¼ cup curaçao
- ¼ cup Grand Marnier
- Grated rind of an orange
- 5 whites from medium-sized eggs (1 cup)

For detailed information about making soufflés, first read the recipe for chocolate soufflé on page 72.

1. Place the orange juice and sugar in a saucepan and cook at a simmer about 10 to 12 minutes or until the sugar has dissolved.

2. Melt the butter in a heavy saucepan over medium heat and blend in the flour and salt. Cook for a few minutes without browning. Pour in the hot orange juice and stir well. Add the curaçao, Grand Marnier and orange rind and let cook for about a minute. Remove the saucepan from the heat.

3. Beat the egg yolks lightly and stir them into the sauce. Strain the sauce into a bowl and cover lightly with waxed paper. Set in a warm place for 15 to 30 minutes.

4. Preheat the oven to 450°F for 15 minutes.

5. Beat the egg whites to soft peaks. Gently, but thoroughly, fold the sauce into the beaten whites, and spoon the mixture into a heated 2-quart soufflé dish, filling it about three-fourths full.

6. Place the soufflé in the preheated oven. Lower the heat to 400°F and cook for 15 minutes. Before serving the soufflé you can, if you like, spoon 2 teaspoons of Grand Marnier on top of it and then sift on a light dusting of powdered sugar. Serve with the following sauce.

Orange Sauce

This is a very simple sauce that adds zest to the soufflé without extra richness.

- ⅔ cup orange juice
- 3" strip dried orange peel
- 3 tablespoons sugar

1. Place the ingredients in a small saucepan and let them simmer for about 10 minutes. Serve warm with the soufflé.

Sautéed Scallops with a Ring of White Rice

~ ─────── ~

- 1½ to 2 pounds bay scallops
- 1 scant teaspoon salt
- ¼ teaspoon cayenne pepper
- ½ tablespoon freshly cut chervil or parsley
- ½ stick butter (2 ounces) at room temperature
- 3 cups cooked white rice (page 24)

1. Prepare the scallops by spreading them out on a sheet of wax paper. Wipe off with a damp cloth any chips of shell or sand that may be clinging to them.

2. Scallops are very tender and should be prepared quickly, so place the ingredients needed for this recipe close at hand.

3. Before cooking the scallops, which will take only about 4 or 5 minutes, prepare the rice ring. Butter a 5-cup ring mold and pack it with 3 cups of hot steamed rice. Place a round serving dish over the top and, holding it and the mold securely, quickly invert them. Remove the mold.

4. To prepare the scallops, first heat a heavy-bottomed 12" skillet over medium heat. When it is hot, add a half stick of butter, raise the heat, and bring the butter to the foaming stage. When the butter begins to brown, add the scallops. Increase the heat and, holding the pan a little above the burner, shake it back and forth over the heat for 3 or 4 minutes. Sprinkle over the cayenne pepper and salt.

5. Fill the center of the rice ring with the scallops and garnish with the chervil or parsley. Serve hot.

Beef with Onions and Red Wine

- **2½ pounds rolled chuck (order the cut used for chicken steak)**
- **1 stick butter**
- **½ pound onions plus 1 medium-sized onion, coarsely grated**
- **1 bay leaf**
- **1 teaspoon thyme**
- **1½ teaspoons freshly ground black pepper**
- **2 tablespoons butter**
- **2¼ cups good, dry red wine**
- **2 tablespoons flour mixed with ½ cup water**
- **2 tablespoons tightly packed brown sugar**
- **1 onion stuck with 2 whole cloves**
- **1 teaspoon salt**
- **2 tablespoons butter**
- **10 white onions**
- **Garnish of freshly cut parsley**

1. Sauté the ½ pound of grated onions with the bay leaf and thyme in a half stick of butter, but do not allow them to brown. When the onions appear transparent, transfer them to a 2-quart casserole.

2. Wipe the rolled chuck with a clean cloth and, using a very sharp knife, cut the meat into 2-inch cubes. Sprinkle with the black pepper and the grated medium-sized onion.

3. Heat a 10" skillet, add 2 tablespoons of butter, and as the foaming stage begins to subside, place 5 or 6 pieces of chuck in the pan at a time, browning them evenly on all sides. Add the browned pieces of beef to the casserole with the sautéed onions.

4. Wipe clean the skillet, pour in the wine and heat until it is very hot; then flame it in order to burn off all the alcohol. Lower the heat of the burner and keep tilting the pan to insure that all the alcohol is burned off; when this is completed, the flame will go out. Pour the wine into the casserole.

5. Add the flour mixture, 1 tablespoon of brown sugar, and the 1 onion stuck with the cloves. Cover and mix the ingredients by firmly shaking the casserole. Place the casserole, still covered, in a 250°F oven.

6. After 1½ hours add a teaspoon of salt.

7. Allow 2½ hours of cooking time in the oven (or longer, depending on the tenderness of the meat). Twenty minutes before the stew is finished cooking, in a 9" skillet heat 2 tablespoons of butter to the foaming stage, sprinkle in a table-spoon of brown sugar, and tilt the pan over the heat until it has blended with the butter. Add the 10 white onions and, keeping the pan very hot, hold it slightly above the heat, shaking and tilting it until the onions are evenly browned. This takes about 8 to 10 minutes. Using a slot-ted spoon, remove the onions and place them on top of the meat in the casserole.

8. Cook uncovered for the final 20 minutes. Spoon off any fat that appears on the surface. Garnish with freshly cut parsley just before serving.

NOTE: After peeling the onions, cut a cross into the bottom of each onion with a sharply pointed knife. This will prevent the onion centers from slipping out while cooking.

Noodles

- 2 eggs
- 1½ cups all-purpose flour
- ½ teaspoon salt
- 5 quarts boiling water
- 1 tablespoon salt
- ¼ cup melted butter

1. Measure the flour and salt and place in a large mixing bowl. Make a well in the center of the flour for the eggs.

2. Lightly beat the eggs and pour them into the center of the flour. With your hands, mix together the eggs and flour. The dough will be very stiff; in order to thoroughly incorporate the flour with the eggs and achieve a smooth dough, the easiest way to handle it is to knead it.

3. Turn the dough out onto a floured board. Don't be alarmed if at this point the dough looks as though it will never adhere together.

4. Knead for about 8 to 10 minutes, making fists with your hands and pressing down on the dough with a rocking motion.

5. When you finish kneading, the dough will be smooth and dry. Cover it lightly with a linen towel and let it rest for about 15 to 20 minutes before rolling it out.

6. Keep rolling until the dough completely loses its elasticity and remains flat and in place. With the first few rollings, you will notice that as soon as it is rolled out the dough will begin to shrink back. Re-flour the board if the dough begins to stick. Roll out the dough as thin as possible—about an eighth of an inch. When rolled out, the dough will be about 27" square, so be sure to flour an area large enough to accommodate it.

7. Cut the dough in strips ¼" to ½" wide. An easy way to do this is to lay a yardstick across the dough as a guide for cutting. Use a dough cutter or a large sharp knife to cut the noodles. After cutting the strips, cut them in half crosswise.

8. Cover the noodles lightly with a linen towel and let them dry for about an hour before cooking. They can be made several hours in advance if you wish.

9. To cook them, bring 5 quarts of water to a full boil. Add 1 tablespoon of salt before plunging in the noodles. Boil them rapidly for 15 to 17 minutes, then test them by tasting.

10. Drain the noodles into a large colander and turn them into a heated casserole or serving dish. Pour over ¼ cup of melted butter, then shake the casserole until all the noodles are coated with the

butter. This prevents them from sticking together in clumps.

NOTE: Served with a simple tomato sauce, or tossed with a half pint of hot heavy cream, butter, and lots of freshly grated Parmesan cheese, these noodles also make a fine luncheon dish accompanied with a green salad, crusty bread, and a light red wine.

Apricot Custard Tart

- ½ **pound dried apricots**
- ¼ **cup sugar**
- 2" **strip lemon peel**
- 2 **cups water**
- 1 9" **tart shell (p. 21)**
- ½ **cup apricot preserves**

1. For this easy and elegant dessert, the apricots and the custard can each be prepared a day in advance.

2. Place the dried apricots in a heavy-bottomed enameled saucepan (or any pan that does not discolor), and let them soak in the 2 cups of water with the lemon peel. Some brands of pre-packaged apricots do not require soaking. I like to use apricots that are unsulphured and without additives; these are usually sold in bulk and do need to be softened by soaking.

3. After 2 hours of soaking, add the sugar and place the saucepan over medium heat. Bring to a simmer, lower the heat, and let cook quietly until tender (about 15 minutes). With a slotted spoon remove the apricots to a dish and reserve any liquid that remains in the saucepan to use later for a glaze.

4. If you can't get unsulphured apricots and have to use the pre-packaged variety, cook them according to the instructions on the package.

5. While the apricots are soaking, you can prepare the dough for the tart shell (see page 21) and make the custard.

Custard

- 1½ **cups milk**
- 2 **tablespoons flour**
- ½ **cup granulated sugar**
- ⅛ **teaspoon salt**
- 4 **egg yolks**
- 2 **tablespoons brandy or 2 teaspoons vanilla extract**

1. To make the custard, first measure the sugar, flour, and salt and stir together in a small bowl. Add about ⅓ cup of the milk and stir until well blended. Add the remaining milk, stir, and pour the mixture into a saucepan.

2. Lightly beat the egg yolks and put them aside.

3. Place the saucepan over medium heat for 4 to 5 minutes, stirring all the while.

When steam begins to rise from the surface, remove the saucepan from the burner.

4. Gradually pour the hot milk mixture into the beaten yolks, stirring rapidly with a wire whisk.

5. Set aside to cool. When cool, flavor the custard with the brandy or vanilla extract.

6. Roll out the tart dough and bake in a preheated 360°F oven until it has lightly browned.

7. When the tart shell has cooled, preheat the oven to 350°F.

8. Heat the apricot preserves until they are pliable enough to spread. If you have enough syrup remaining (about a half cup) after cooking the apricots, use it in place of the preserves, boiling it until it thickens. Paint the bottom and sides of the tart with the apricot glaze. This glazing keeps the crust from getting too soggy.

9. Arrange the apricots in a single layer, reserving three of the most attractive ones. Pour over the custard, and place the reserved apricots in the center of the tart.

10. Set in the middle rack of the oven and bake for 15 to 20 minutes until the custard appears set. This tart is most flavorful when it is served at room temperature.

Roast Veal Garnished with Carrots and Mushrooms

The best cut for roast veal is the top of the round. This is the same part of the leg from which veal scallops are cut and is ideal, as it has no fat, tendons, or gristle. Because this section is only about 2½ to 3 pounds in weight, the roast will be small, but there is no waste and a roast this size will easily serve six people. (This cut of veal is sometimes difficult to find. As we mentioned in the recipe for veal scallops, a European-style butcher shop is usually the best place to shop for it.)

- **2½ to 3 pounds top round of veal**
- **½ stick soft butter plus 3 tablespoons for mushroom garnish**
- **¼ teaspoon dried thyme or sprig of fresh thyme**
- **3 carrots, sliced lengthwise**
- **Freshly ground pepper**
- **2 tablespoons heavy cream**
- **½ pound mushrooms**

1. Preheat the oven at 300°F for 15 minutes.

2. Cook the roast in a heavy 2-quart casserole with a close-fitting cover. Veal tends to be dry, and cooking it this way will help keep the meat tender and moist.

3. Wipe the veal with a damp cloth and spread 2 tablespoons of the soft butter over it.

4. Arrange the carrots in the bottom of the casserole. Grate pepper over the veal

and sprinkle it with the dried thyme. (If you have fresh thyme, place the sprigs with the carrots.) Cover the casserole and set it in the center of the preheated oven for 2 hours.

5. Fifteen minutes before the end of the roasting time, remove the veal and pour off the juices into a Pyrex pitcher or bowl. Before returning the veal to the oven for the final cooking, smooth a tablespoon of the soft butter over the top. Leave off the cover if more browning is desired.

6. Skim off the fat from the pan juices and strain the juices into a 9" skillet. Bring to a boil over medium heat and boil rapidly until the liquid is reduced by half. Stir in 2 tablespoons of heavy cream and taste for seasoning.

7. Sauté the mushrooms for garnishing the veal (see mushroom garnish, page 17).

8. When the veal has been sliced for serving, arrange the mushrooms around the meat. Reheat the sauce briefly and ladle several spoonfuls over the veal, reserving some sauce to pass at the table.

Crêpes Suzette

All types of pancakes made just before serving are superior to those prepared in advance, which generally fall flat. However, I find that this batter, which is richer than most crêpe batters, allows one to cook pancakes that will retain their light, springy texture even when cooked 3 to 4 hours before serving. Both the crêpe batter and the orange butter can be prepared a day ahead or several hours in advance, and the pancakes can be made in the afternoon. All that remains to be done at dinner time to complete this very special dessert is to reheat the crêpes in the orange butter; and this can be done in a chafing dish at the table, if you like.

Crêpe Batter

- 6 tablespoons all-purpose flour
- 2 whole eggs plus 2 yolks
- 1 cup heavy cream
- 1 cup milk
- 2 tablespoons granulated sugar
- 1 tablespoon melted butter
- 2 teaspoons curaçao

1. To make the batter, first sift the flour into a mixing bowl. Add the eggs and yolks and enough cream to make a smooth paste. Stir in the sugar, melted butter, and curaçao and mix well. Add the remaining cream, blend, and then refrigerate the batter from 3 hours to overnight.

Orange Butter

- 1 stick butter
- 5 tablespoons superfine sugar
- Grated rind of 2 tangerines or oranges

- ½ teaspoon lemon juice
- 2 tablespoons fresh tangerine or orange juice
- ½ teaspoon curaçao

1. To prepare the orange butter, place the softened butter with the sugar and the grated rind in a small bowl. Add the juice and curaçao. Cream the ingredients together with the back of a spoon until they are well blended. Because oranges vary in flavor during different seasons, taste the batter to see if it has enough zest. If it seems lacking in flavor, add a few drops of orange bitters or a little more grated rind. Cover the bowl well and keep in the refrigerator.

2. To cook the crêpes, use a 4" or 5" crêpe pan (this recipe will make 24 five-inch crêpes). Heat the pan until it is hot and rub over sweet butter or oil. One greasing is usually enough.

3. Spoon about 2 tablespoons of batter into the center of the pan and quickly tilt the pan around to cover the bottom. Cook the pancakes over a medium flame. Turn them over when the surface appears dry, or after about 10 seconds (these crêpes will brown much faster than those on page 110).

4. As they will also cook in the sauce, cook them for only 3 to 5 seconds on the second side, and then turn them out onto a cookie sheet.

5. To turn a pancake, lift the pan off the burner, tilting it so that it is almost vertical. Using a short straight spatula, loosen the crêpe around the top edge until it begins to fall away from the pan. Lift it up with the spatula or with your fingertips and carefully turn over. If it falls unevenly into the pan, just lift it up and lay it straight.

6. As the pancakes cool slightly on the cookie sheet, you can place them in stacks; they won't stick together. When all the pancakes have been made, cover the stacks lightly with waxed paper to keep them from drying out.

7. Just before serving, heat a wide, heavy-bottomed skillet and place in about 3 tablespoons of the orange butter. You don't want the crêpes swimming in butter; the edges should be crisp. Add more butter as it is needed. Tilt the pan back and forth to spread the butter over the whole surface of the pan until it is bubbling. Quickly put in 4 crêpes with the lighter side face down. After a few seconds, turn them over, using a small spatula and the back of a serving spoon. As soon as you turn them, begin folding them—first in half, then in quarters. As they are folded into quarters, stack them on one side of the pan.

For Flaming

- 1 liqueur glass of curaçao
- 1 liqueur glass of high-proof Jamaican rum or brandy

1. Warm the curaçao and rum or brandy over low heat. When all the crêpes have been folded, sprinkle with the heated curaçao and the rum or brandy. Set alight and serve the crêpes as soon as the flame dies down.

Edna Lewis in August of 1984, at the annual Bethel Baptist Church revival in Unionville, Virginia, near the site of her hometown of Freetown.

Luncheon Menus

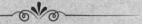

Shrimp Sautéed in Butter with Herbs (p. 93)
White Rice (p. 24)
Mixed Green Salad
French Bread
Fresh Raspberries and Cream

Cheese Soufflé (p. 93)
Romaine Lettuce with French Dressing (p. 12)
French Bread
Babka (p. 94)
Basket of Fresh Pears
Coffee

Grilled Veal Kidneys with Seasoned Butter Sauce (p. 96)
Endive and Watercress with French Dressing (p. 12)
Crusty Rolls
Butter
Chilled Compote of Orange Slices (p. 97)
Coffee

Quiche Lorraine (p. 97)
Salad of Mixed Greens
Basket of Fresh Fruit
Sugar Cookies (p. 98)
Coffee

Pan-Broiled Quail (p. 99)
Spoon Bread (p. 100)
Butter
Salad of Watercress and Endive
Poached Pears (p. 100)
Cats' Tongues (p. 101)
Coffee

❦

Cold Poached Chicken (p. 102)
Herb Mayonnaise (p. 15)
Green Beans Vinaigrette (p. 103)
Hot Buttered French Bread
Poached Fresh Peaches (p. 103)
Pound Cake (p. 104)
Coffee

Shrimp Sautéed in Butter with Herbs on a Ring of White Rice

~~~~~~~~~~~~~~~~~~~~~~~~~~~~~~~

- 2 pounds shrimp, shelled and deveined
- ½ stick butter
- ¼ clove garlic
- ½ large lemon
- 1 tablespoon parsley, freshly cut
- Salt and pepper to taste
- 3 cups cooked white rice

~~~~~~~~~~~~~~~~~~~~~~~~~~~~~~~

1. Butter a 5-cup ring mold and pack it with hot steamed rice that has been cooked by the method suggested on page 24. Place a round serving dish over the top and, holding it and the mold securely, quickly invert them. Remove the mold and set the ring in a warm spot.

2. To prepare the shrimp, heat a 12" skillet over medium heat. When it is hot, add a half stick of butter, raise the heat, bring the butter to the foaming stage, and add the garlic. When the butter begins to brown, add the shrimp in one layer and cook over medium-high heat. When they begin to turn pink (in about 2 to 3 minutes), turn them. Add the parsley and squeeze over the lemon. Sauté 2 or 3 minutes more.

3. Spoon the shrimp into the center of the ring and pour over the sauce.

Cheese Soufflé

~~~~~~~~~~~~~~~~~~~~~~~~~~~~~~~

- ½ ounce or 4 tablespoons Parmesan cheese
- 5 ounces white cheddar
- 3 ounces Swiss Gruyère (not processed)
- 2 tablespoons butter
- 2 tablespoons flour
- 1 cup warm milk
- 3 egg yolks
- 5 egg whites
- ½ teaspoon salt
- 1 teaspoon dry mustard
- ¼ teaspoon cayenne pepper

~~~~~~~~~~~~~~~~~~~~~~~~~~~~~~~

1. See the note on soufflés on page 72.

2. Grate the cheeses, using the next to finest side of a 4-sided grater.

3. Melt the butter in a heavy saucepan over medium heat. Add the flour and cook a few minutes until the flour is well blended but has not browned.

4. Pour in the warm milk, stirring all the while. Remove the pan from the burner

and add the yolks, slightly beaten. Mix in well, return the pan to the burner, and stir a minute or two.

5. Remove the saucepan from the burner and thoroughly combine the grated cheeses with the sauce. Add the spices. If the cheese is finely grated, it will dissolve from the heat of the sauce and will not need further cooking on top of the stove.

6. Cover the pan lightly with waxed paper and set in a warm place.

7. Beat the egg whites to soft peaks; stir the cheese batter well to soften it up before you gently but thoroughly fold in the whites.

8. Spoon the mixture into a 1½-quart soufflé dish that has been heated for a few minutes in the oven. Set the dish in the oven, raise the thermostat to 475°F for 3 or 4 minutes, then turn it back to 450°F. Cook for a total of 15 minutes and serve at once.

9. Plan to finish the soufflé within 20 minutes of completing the sauce, as the cheese will stiffen if the sauce becomes cold.

Babka

Dough

- 1 package dry yeast or 1 yeast cake
- 2 teaspoons sugar
- 2 cups all-purpose, unbleached flour
- ½ cup lukewarm milk
- 4 eggs, lightly beaten
- 1 scant teaspoon salt
- 1½ sticks soft sweet butter

1. Place the yeast, sugar, and 3 tablespoons of the flour in a warm 2- to 3-quart mixing bowl and mix well. Sprinkle with the warm milk, and set the bowl in a warm, draft-free place until the mixture becomes foamy or bubbly, which will take 15 to 20 minutes.

2. Add the lightly beaten eggs, flour and salt, and stir well until the batter becomes smooth.

3. Add the softened butter and stir until the dough is smooth and elastic (about 5 minutes). Turn it into a shallow bowl, and chill in the refrigerator overnight or place in the freezer for 4 to 5 hours.

Filling

- ⅔ cup walnuts
- ⅔ cup seedless raisins
- ½ cup raspberry preserves
- 2 teaspoons cinnamon
- ⅔ cup superfine sugar
- 2 egg whites

1. To prepare the ingredients for the filling, chop the nuts and cut the raisins in half. Mix the cinnamon with the sugar. If the preserves are stiff, and they usually are, stir them well to make

them more pliable. Beat the egg whites to soft peaks.

2. Cut off 2 sheets of waxed paper each about 22 inches long. Spread them out with the sheet nearest you overlapping the second one. Dust them generously with flour.

3. From this point, work swiftly as the dough is rich and fragile.

4. Place the dough on the paper, and roll out with a cold, flour-dusted rolling pin. As you roll, pick the dough up frequently and give it a quarter turn. If it begins to stick dust the sticky spot with additional flour. Roll the dough into a rectangular shape approximately 18" x 12" and ¼" thick.

5. Spread the egg white over the dough to within about 2" from the edges. Quickly sprinkle with the cinnamon sugar, then the raisins and nuts. Drop about 8 or 10 dollops of the raspberry jam over the filling.

6. Now roll the dough up in jelly-roll fashion. To do this, lift up the edge of waxed paper closest to you and give it a quick flip away from you to begin rolling up the dough. Give the dough about three turns. Flip the far edge of the paper toward you. With a good grasp on each end of the paper holding the rolled-up dough, shape the roll into a horseshoe. Then lift it up and carefully slide it into a tube pan 10" long and 3" deep, paper and all. Gently pull the paper out from the dough; it should slide out very easily.

7. Hold the mold with the two ends of the horseshoe-shaped dough away from you. Join them by tilting the pan and shaking it gently. With a rubber spatula or the back of a spoon, lightly press down the dough from around the sides of the tube pan so that the ring settles evenly on the bottom. Brush 1 tablespoon of melted butter over the top.

8. Set the pan in a warm (about 80°) draft-free place to rise to within ½" from the top. This will take about 1 to 1½ hours.

9. Allow 15 minutes to preheat the oven to 375°F.

10. Bake the babka about 45 minutes. Remove and set the pan on a rack for 12 minutes before turning it out onto a serving plate.

Grilled Veal Kidneys with Seasoned Butter Sauce

Grilled Veal Kidneys

- 4 small veal kidneys
- ½ stick soft butter
- 1 tablespoon finely cut parsley
- ¼ lemon
- Salt and ground black pepper

Buy small or medium-small kidneys and ask your butcher to leave them in the fat.

Seasoned Butter Sauce

- 1 stick soft butter
- 2 teaspoons finely cut chervil
- 1 teaspoon finely cut parsley
- ¼ teaspoon lemon juice
- Salt and white pepper

1. Prepare the seasoned butter sauce by blending together the ingredients a few hours in advance.

2. Just before grilling prepare the kidneys. Cut a slit through the fat to the kidney. With your fingers, pull off the fat and membrane. Cut away any fat attached to the center of the kidney.

3. Slice the kidneys through lengthwise almost in half and flatten them out butterfly style. With a small sharp knife, cut away any excess fat.

4. Wash the kidneys well under running cold water and pat dry with a towel.

5. Paint both sides of each kidney with the soft butter and set them aside.

6. Preheat the broiler for 5 minutes.

7. Sprinkle the kidneys with salt and grind the black pepper over them. Place them cut side up on the broiler pan and squeeze the juice of the lemon over the kidneys.

8. Kidneys tend to curl up under heat, so place a heavy wire rack over them. An excellent rack for grilling kidneys is a long-handled hinged grill with medium grids of the type that is generally used for outdoor grilling of fish or steaks.

9. Place the kidneys 3 or 4 inches below medium-high heat. Cook about 4 minutes on each side. Kidneys should be crisp around the edges, yet juicy when you cut into them, so take care not to overcook them.

10. Remove the kidneys to a hot serving dish and garnish with the fresh parsley. Serve hot with the butter sauce.

Chilled Compote of Orange Slices

- 3 large navel oranges
- 2 2" pieces dried orange peel (See note on dried orange peel in Nutmeg Sauce recipe, page 51)
- ½ cup sugar
- 1 cup water

1. Peel the oranges and, with a sharp knife, carefully remove all of the white pith. Cut oranges into slices about ³⁄₁₆" thick and remove any seeds.

2. Bring the sugar, water, and orange peel to a boil in a Pyrex, enamel, or stainless saucepan, and cook briskly for 7 minutes. Remove from the burner and place the orange slices in the hot syrup.

3. When cool, cover and place in the refrigerator until chilled. Remove the orange peel before serving.

Quiche Lorraine

Pie Crust

- 1½ cups sifted flour
- ⅔ stick butter, cut into small pieces
- ¼ teaspoon salt
- 4 tablespoons cold water

1. Place the flour, salt, and chilled butter pieces in a bowl and cut with a pastry blender until the mixture has the texture of cornmeal.

2. Sprinkle the cold water quickly over the surface, mix with a large spoon, and pull the dough together lightly. Gently shape into a ball with your fingers, and place the dough in the refrigerator. Let stand 20 to 30 minutes before rolling it out.

3. Lightly flour the rolling pin and board and roll out the dough to fit into an 11" x 8" baking pan or an 11" pie dish. Roll up the dough onto the pin and then carefully unroll it over the pie dish, shaping it gently into the bottom and sides. Cover the pie dish with waxed paper and return it to the refrigerator while you prepare the filling.

4. Preheat the oven to 375°F.

Filling

- ½ pound bacon
- ½ pound Gruyère cheese (not processed), finely grated
- 3 eggs
- 1 pint heavy cream
- ⅛ teaspoon cayenne pepper
- ½ teaspoon salt (or to taste)

1. Place the bacon slices in a flat baking pan and set it in the middle rack of the preheated oven and cook about 15 minutes or until the bacon is light brown. Place the cooked bacon on paper toweling to drain.

NOTE: Don't cook the bacon too far in advance; otherwise the flavor will go stale and it won't crumble easily.

2. Lower the oven temperature to 350°F.

3. Beat the eggs lightly. Stir in the cream, salt, and cayenne. Mix well and strain.

4. Sprinkle the grated cheese over the surface of the dough. Spoon in the custard carefully so as not to disturb the cheese. Crumble most of the bacon over the custard, reserving a bit for the final garnish.

5. Bake the quiche in the center of the oven for 25 minutes, or until the custard is set and lightly browned.

6. Remove the tart from the oven. Crumble the remaining bacon over the surface.

7. Let the quiche rest for 10 to 12 minutes. This will make it easier to slice. Serve warm.

Sugar Cookies

- 1 stick butter (4 ounces)
- ¾ cup extra-fine sugar
- 2 medium eggs
- 2 cups all-purpose flour, sifted
- 1 teaspoon powdered ginger
- ½ teaspoon baking powder
- 1 tablespoon cream
- ¼ cup crushed cube sugar

1. Cream together the butter and sugar, add the eggs, and mix well.

2. Add the flour that has been sifted with the ginger and baking powder. Then add the cream and mix until well blended. Spoon the dough (it will be very soft) onto a dinner plate and spread it out evenly. Let it rest 45 minutes in the freezer. It is important that this very soft dough be well chilled.

3. Allow 15 minutes to heat the oven to 400°F.

4. Use a cold board and a cold rolling pin for easier rolling. Remove the dough in 3 parts, always leaving the unused portion in the refrigerator. Flour the board and pin and roll the dough quickly so that it is as thin as possible (about the thickness of a quarter). These cookies taste best when rolled thin.

5. Cut with a cookie cutter. When cutting out the cookies, cut them very close; re-rolling leftover trimmings is a wasted effort, as both the texture and flavor will change when you reshape the dough and add more flour. Bake the trimmings as they are, or discard them.

6. Lift the cookies with a thin spatula onto an ungreased cookie sheet. If some cookies are rolled thinner than others,

put the thin ones in the center of the sheet. Sprinkle the cookies with crushed cube sugar and place in a 400°F oven for 8 to 10 minutes.

7. Remove the cookies from the baking sheet while they are still warm, and place them on a wire rack to cool. Store in a tightly covered tin.

Pan-Broiled Quail

Quail, like pheasant, is another feathered game bird that is very popular and plentiful in the Virginia countryside. Although quail are small, they are meaty and tender and cook quickly. Like pheasant, they are also more flavorful after aging.

In urban areas, quail can usually be obtained easily from local butchers, although a day or two advance request may be necessary; or they can be ordered from game farms.

- **4 quail**
- **¼ teaspoon fresh thyme, if available**
- **1 stick butter, plus 2 or 3 thin pats**
- **1 scant teaspoon salt**
- **1 scant teaspoon freshly ground pepper**
- **Garnish of watercress**

1. If the quail are in feather, pluck them, or have your butcher do it. Singe off any fine pin feathers.

2. Wash the birds in cold water and pat them dry. Then split the quail down the back. Remove the entrails and lungs, and wipe the inside cavity with a damp cloth.

3. Flatten the birds with one stroke of a heavy wide-bladed knife. Mix the salt, pepper and thyme. (If the thyme is fresh, cut it finely; if dry, crush it with a pestle or the back of a spoon.) Thoroughly rub both sides of each quail with this mixture.

4. Heat a heavy 12" skillet and place in ¾ stick of butter. Bring it to the foaming stage. When the butter reaches the peak of the foaming and just begins to brown, place in as many quail as will fit without crowding.

5. Sauté the quail on each side for 3 or 4 minutes. Butter a shallow, heavy roasting pan and place the quail in it. Lay a few thin pats of butter on each bird. Cover the pan loosely with a sheet of foil and place it in a 375°F preheated oven. Roast for 30 minutes, basting once or twice with the remaining butter.

6. Remove the quail to a hot platter and place in the oven for a few minutes while you finish the sauce.

7. If the pan juices are too scant, add ¼ cup of hot water. Scrape a spoon over the bottom of the pan to loosen any particles clinging to it. Season to taste with salt and pepper. Strain through a medium sieve and pour the sauce around, the platter of quail. Garnish with watercress.

Spoon Bread

~

- **1 cup white water-ground cornmeal**
- **2 cups milk**
- **2 tablespoons baking powder**
- **½ teaspoon salt**
- **2 eggs, separated**
- **2 tablespoons butter melted in a 1½ quart Pyrex dish**

1. Preheat the oven to 375°F.
2. Sift the cornmeal and salt into a mixing bowl, add one cup of milk, mix, and let stand 10 or more minutes to absorb.
3. Add the egg yolks, slightly beaten, stir well, and add the melted butter from the Pyrex dish. Place the empty Pyrex dish into the oven to heat.
4. Add the second cup of milk, the baking powder, and the egg whites, beaten to near-soft peaks. This is a very liquid batter, so don't be concerned about its appearance at this stage.
5. Remove the Pyrex dish from the oven; pour in the batter and set it back into the oven to cook for 35 to 40 minutes. Serve hot as you would a soufflé, and pass with lots of butter.

Poached Pears

~

You may serve these pears warm or cold, but we recommend serving them warm as we think they are especially flavorful that way, and the aroma of the freshly cooked pears mingled with the vanilla is just too good to chill.

- **4 ripe, sweet Bartlett pears**
- **2 cups cold water**
- **1½ cups granulated sugar**
- **½ plump vanilla bean**

1. Combine the water, sugar, and vanilla bean in a Pyrex, enamel, or stainless-steel saucepan large enough to hold 8 pear halves. Bring to a boil over medium heat and let simmer while you prepare the pears.
2. Peel, slice in half, and core the pears. Place each pear immediately into the syrup with the cut side down as soon as it has been prepared. This will insure an attractive, clear appearance. Pears tend to float, and their exposed parts turn brown.
3. Carefully turn the pears over with a wooden spoon after about 20 minutes.
4. Poach the pears about 40 minutes. Don't let the syrup boil or the pears may fall apart. When the pears begin to look slightly transparent, use a toothpick to

test for doneness. The pears are cooked if a toothpick goes right through the fruit without any resistance. Another way to test that will avoid putting lots of holes in the pears is to lift out half a pear and press it gently between your thumb and forefinger. If it feels somewhat soft, the pears are done.

Cats' Tongues

Fresh ingredients are essential for all baking, but these cookies are especially delicate in flavor; and stale powdered ginger or flour would spoil their taste.

- ⅔ cup all-purpose flour
- 1⅓ cups powdered sugar
- 1 teaspoon powdered ginger
- ½ cup heavy cream
- Whites of 2 large eggs

1. Preheat the oven to 400°F.
2. Rub 3 cookie sheets with sweet butter. Sift both the flour and the powdered sugar before measuring. Combine the flour, sugar, and ginger, and sift together.
3. Whip the cream just until it is frothy, and whip the egg whites to the same stage. Mix the cream and egg whites together. Spoon into the flour mixture and stir in a circular motion until the batter is well blended.
4. Place a cookie sheet close to the bowl of batter. Dip in a dinner knife and give the knife a turn, which should gather about a good teaspoon of the batter onto the blade. Strike a mark on the cookie sheet and end it with a thin line. It should form a cookie about 2½" long.
5. These cookies will spread, so allow about 1½" between each one. When you have filled each cookie sheet, place it in the middle rack of the oven for 7 minutes. When the edges are brown, the cookies are done.
6. Remove from the oven and let them cool for 2 or 3 minutes. Then slip a thin spatula carefully under each cookie, removing them before they cool too much and harden to the cookie sheet. (If this happens, set them back into the oven for 2 or 3 minutes more to soften.)
7. Place the cookies on a wire rack, and when they have cooled, store them in an airtight tin.

Cold Poached Chicken

⌇⌇ ⎯⎯⎯ ⌇⌇

This is a wonderful dish to serve for lunch or Sunday night supper during warm summer weather, as it is light yet piquant in flavor when served with herb mayonnaise and green beans vinaigrette. It is also pleasing to the eye on a hot day because of its bed of lettuce garnished with the green beans and watercress. And, sometimes of especial importance in summer, there is the added convenience of being able to prepare the chicken and its accompaniments in advance.

Chicken

- **2 chickens, 3 to 3½ pounds each**
- **2 teaspoons salt**
- **1 teaspoon black pepper**
- **Romaine lettuce, enough to cover serving platter**
- **Garnish of watercress**

1. Wash the chickens inside and out and pat them dry. Rub the inside cavities with a mixture of the salt and pepper. Tie the legs together. Place the chickens in a heavy casserole or pot just large enough to hold them.

Poaching Stock

- **1½ cups cold water**
- **½ cup dry white wine or vermouth**
- **1 stalk celery with the leaves**
- **Few sprigs parsley**
- **Sprig thyme or ¼ teaspoon dried thyme**

1. Add the ingredients for the poaching stock to the casserole and cover tightly. Set the casserole over medium heat and bring the stock to a simmer. Lower the heat so that the chickens continue to cook at just under a simmer for 45 minutes to an hour when they should be tender.

2. Cool the chickens in the stock. Remove and tilt them to drain off juices from the inside cavities. Place them on a platter to further drain for about 15 minutes, then cover and place in the refrigerator.

3. Before serving, cut off the wings (don't serve the wings as they have very little meat on this size chicken) and the legs. Remove the skin from the breast as it is not especially attractive and it is easier to slice the chicken without it. For thin, even slices I find a sharp knife with a wide blade most useful.

4. Arrange the chickens on a bed of romaine lettuce. Garnish with green beans vinaigrette (prepared from the following recipe) and sprigs of watercress. Serve with a bowl of light mayonnaise (page 15) flavored with finely cut tarragon and watercress or parsley.

Green Beans Vinaigrette

- **2 pounds young green beans of equal size**
- **2 teaspoons salt**
- **French dressing (page 12)**

1. Wash, drain, and snip off the ends of 2 pounds of young green beans of equal size.
2. Fill a 3-quart saucepan three-fourths full with cold water and bring to a boil. Add the beans and 2 teaspoons of salt.

3. Boil the beans uncovered about 5 minutes, or until they are tender, but not soft. Drain, and plunge them into ice water for 1 to 2 minutes to keep them from cooking further.
4. Remove the beans from the ice water and spread them out on paper toweling to dry, then marinate them in French dressing made with lemon juice and a half teaspoon of finely grated onion.

Poached Fresh Peaches

- **4 ripe peaches**
- **2 cups cold water**
- **1½ cups granulated sugar**
- **½ plump vanilla bean**

Poached peaches can be prepared a day in advance of serving, if desired.

1. Combine the water, sugar, and vanilla bean in a Pyrex, enamel, or stainless-steel saucepan large enough to hold 8 peach halves. Bring to a boil over medium heat and let simmer while you prepare the peaches.

2. Peel, slice in half, and pit the peaches. Place each peach half into the syrup with the cut side down as soon as it has been peeled and halved so as to prevent them from discoloring.
3. Cook the peaches about 40 minutes. Don't let the syrup boil as this might result in peaches with ragged edges, or worse, the fruit might fall apart.
4. Halfway through the cooking, carefully turn the peaches over with a wooden spoon.
5. Cool the peaches in the syrup and place in the refrigerator to chill before serving.

Pound Cake

〜—————〜

The special feature of this cake is that it improves with age. The time spent in making it is well rewarded. I always mix a pound cake by hand with a wooden spoon, using a circular stirring motion. If you use an electric mixer, follow the speeds suggested by the manufacturer. Too high a speed will develop too much heat in the bowl and cause the butter to become too soft, a disastrous development for this particular cake.

- 1⅔ cups extra-fine granulated sugar
- 2 sticks sweet butter (1 cup)
- 5 medium or 4 large eggs (cold)
- 2 cups minus 2 tablespoons all-purpose flour
- 1 scant teaspoon salt
- 1 teaspoon almond extract
- 1 teaspoon vanilla

1. Preheat the oven to 300°F.
2. Butter the bottom of a 9" x 3½" tube pan and dust it lightly with flour.
3. Cream the butter until it appears waxy or shiny. Add the sugar gradually, stirring thoroughly until the mixture has the texture of hard sauce.
4. Add the eggs one at a time, stirring after each addition until the butter returns to "hard-sauce" firmness. (The use of cold eggs chills the butter and keeps the mixture firm.)
5. Sift the flour twice, add the salt, and sift once more. Add the flour to the butter-sugar mixture in 4 portions, stirring well after each addition. At this point all traces of sugar granules should have disappeared.

6. Mix in the extracts, then spoon the batter into the tube pan. The batter should almost hold its shape when spooned into the pan.
7. Bake for 35 minutes at 300°F. Then raise the oven temperature to 325°F for the next 25 minutes. Long, slow baking tends to dry out a cake. This is why we increase the oven temperature once the batter has risen close to the top of the pan. (It will continue to rise slightly during the final 25 minutes.)
8. After 1 hour, test for doneness (see page 25). If the cake is not quite done, continue baking; but check it every few minutes, as butter cakes dry out when overbaked.
9. Remove the cake from the oven and run a spatula or knife around the sides of the pan. Gently turn the cake out onto a cake rack, place a second rack over the cake, and quickly invert it. Leave the cake on the rack to cool, covering it lightly with a large linen or paper napkin to prevent it from drying.
10. Store pound cake in a clean, odorless cake tin.

Special
organic
Cauli.
2.00 lb

Edna Lewis in 1989 at the Gage & Tollner Restaurant in Brooklyn, New
York, where she was chef for five years before her retirement in the mid-1990s.

Buffet Dinners

Beef Stroganoff (p. 109)
Wild Rice (p. 17)
Salad of Mixed Greens
Hot Buttered French Bread
Dessert Crêpes (p. 110)
Coffee

Shrimp Curry (p. 111) or Chicken Curry (p. 114) with White Rice
Chutney (p. 115)
Crisp Cucumber Salad (p. 116)
Crème Caramel Filled with Whipped Cream and
Topped with Pistachio Nuts (p. 117)
Coffee

Chicken À La Kiev (p. 118)
Wild Rice (p. 17)
Mushroom Sauce (p. 119)
Romaine Lettuce and Italian Watercress Salad
Hot Buttered French Bread
Assorted Cheeses
Fresh Fruit Bowl
Cats' Tongues (p. 101)
Coffee

Beef Stroganoff

(For 12 to 14 people)

- **4 pounds filet of beef (or bottom round or rump steak)**
- **3 medium onions**
- **½ stick butter (2 ounces)**
- **⅓ cup beef broth (beef bouillon)**
- **4 tablespoons tomato purée**
- **1½ cups heavy cream**
- **1 teaspoon salt**
- **2 teaspoons sweet paprika**
- **1 stick butter**
- **1½ pounds mushrooms, cleaned and halved**
- **1 teaspoon freshly ground black pepper**
- **2 tablespoons lemon juice**
- **½ cup sour cream**

1. Ask your butcher to cut the beef in strips 2" long and about ¼" in diameter and thickness. Once cut, the meat will begin to bleed, so if you are not going to use it within an hour or so, buy it in one piece and, with a sharp heavy French chef's knife, cut it in strips just before preparing the stroganoff.

2. Grate the onions, using the coarse section of a grater. Heat a skillet (I prefer one of heavy aluminum) and bring a half stick of butter to the point just past the peak of the foaming stage, then sauté the onions for 8 to 10 minutes without allowing them to brown. Next add the bouillon and tomato purée, mixing well. Let this simmer for a few minutes and then add the heavy cream, continuing to simmer for another 5 minutes. Strain the sauce through a Foley mill into a warm casserole that has been placed over a pan of hot but not boiling water. Stir in the teaspoon of salt and the 2 teaspoons of sweet paprika.

3. In a clean skillet heat ¼ stick of butter to the same point as for the onions, and begin to sauté the meat. (Do not put in too many pieces at one time or the meat will steam.) Brown the strips of beef quickly on both sides (about 1½ minutes) and, using a slotted spoon, stir the finished pieces into the sauce. The heavy cream sauce will seal the meat so that it will be plump and juicy when served.

4. If the butter remaining in the pan has not burned, add ¾ stick of butter and heat until very hot. Add the prepared mushrooms and cook over high heat for about 5 minutes, holding the pan slightly above the heat when necessary to prevent burning. While the mushrooms are cooking, add 1 teaspoon of freshly ground black pepper and 2 tablespoons of lemon juice.

5. Stir the mushrooms into the casserole, mixing well, and then taste for seasoning.

6. If the stroganoff is to be served right away, add the sour cream; if you are preparing it in advance, add it after you have reheated the casserole. Adding the sour cream just before serving seems to give this dish a better flavor.

Dessert Crêpes

The great thing about this batter is that it will keep for 3 days; if you have any left over after making your dessert, keep it to use for a special treat at breakfast or afternoon tea.

- ⅓ cup all-purpose flour
- 1 teaspoon sugar
- 2 eggs
- 1 cup milk at room temperature
- 1 teaspoon melted butter
- Granulated sugar
- Assorted preserves

1. Place the flour and sugar in a mixing bowl. Add the eggs and mix with a fork to break up the eggs. Pour in a third of the milk at a time. Add the melted butter. Don't be concerned if all the lumps don't dissolve with stirring; they will do so while the batter is resting.

2. Pour the batter into a pitcher and place it in the refrigerator for at least 2 hours.

3. For these crêpes, you will need a 6" to 7" crêpe pan; that is, a pan with low, sloping sides so that you can easily turn the pancakes. (When you find such a crêpe pan you like, use it only for making the crêpes.)

4. To cook the crêpes, heat the pan until a drop of water sizzles when it hits the pan, then quickly add a dab of butter (about ¼ teaspoon). Turn it out when it foams up and wipe the pan lightly with a paper towel to remove any excess grease. One greasing is usually all that is needed. If you find a pancake sticking, however, butter the pan again.

5. Select a large round spoon that will hold enough batter so that when you pour a spoonful into the center of the hot pan the batter will spread almost to the edge. (Experiment with different-sized spoons until you find the right one for your crêpe pan.)

6. Spoon the batter into the center of the pan and quickly tilt the pan around to cover the bottom. Cook the pancake about 25 to 35 seconds or until the surface appears dry and the edges brown. Turn them quickly with a thin spatula or your fingertips. Cook for 6 to 8 seconds more and turn them out rapidly onto a cookie sheet that has been sprinkled with granulated sugar. As you cook the crêpes, the pan will retain more and more heat and you will find that the remaining pancakes will need even less time to cook.

7. Continue making crêpes until you have enough for all your guests. (Allow about 3 for each serving.)

8. Sprinkle the crêpes with sugar to keep them from sticking and roll them up loosely. Place the crêpes on an oven-proof serving dish and cover lightly with a linen napkin or dishtowel to keep them from drying out. Before serving, heat them for 2 or 3 minutes in a 400°F oven. (The crêpes are very delicate, so be careful not to heat them any longer than this.)

9. Serve the warmed crêpes with assorted preserves. Lingonberry and strawberry preserves slightly warmed are good accompaniments spooned over the rolled-up crêpes. Freshly grated lemon peel is also delicious.

Shrimp Curry

This savory curry is made in three simple steps: the sauce, the shrimp, and a combination of the two.

The quality of the spices you use to prepare curry are very important. Newly purchased spices that have been ground just before use will result in a wonderfully fragrant and flavorful curry. Stale spices are likely to make, at best, a mundane curry; or worse, a musty-tasting one. When you buy spices, note the date of purchase on the container. Most spices will keep for about a year, but should then be discarded. Whole spices, such as cardamon-seed capsules or cuminseed, will keep longer than ground ones. When using whole spices, however, remember to grind them before measuring.

Shrimp

- 2 pounds raw shrimp
- ½ cup shrimp stock
- 1 coconut (see note)
- 2 medium onions
- 1 bunch scallions
- 1 clove garlic
- 6 ³⁄₁₆" slices fresh ginger root
- 12 thin slices cucumber (optional)
- ¼ lemon or ½ lime

1. Shell and devein the shrimp.

2. Make simple stock by cooking a handful of shrimp shells in a cup of water for 10 minutes and then straining.

3. Break open the coconut with a hammer or heavy mallet and discard the liquid. Grate the coconut meat over a bowl, following the directions in the note at end of this recipe.

4. Pour 1 cup of boiling water over the grated meat and let sit for 15 to 20 minutes. Squeeze out the liquid into a bowl by hand, or press the mixture through a sieve. After about 20 minutes a heavy cream will rise to the top. It is this cream that you will use to thicken as well as to flavor the sauce.

5. Next, make the curry powder.

Curry Powder

- 2 teaspoons ground turmeric
- ½ teaspoons cardamon, freshly ground
- 1 teaspoon ground cuminseed
- 1 teaspoon ground chilies, fresh or dried
- 2" piece of Ceylon rolled cinnamon bark

1. Grind the cardamon seeds, the cumin, and the chilies, if they are dried; then measure and set aside. To grind the spices, use a pepper mill or crush them fine with a mortar and pestle.

2. Grate the onions and finely cut the scallions.

3. Heat a half stick of the butter in a skillet until it is just past the peak of the foaming stage. Add the onions and scallions and sauté, without browning, until they are soft.

4. Stir in the ginger, the ground spices, and the piece of cinnamon. Curry powder absorbs lots of fat so add more butter if the mixture seems too thick; you want it to remain soft and pliable. Sauté for 3 or 4 minutes.

5. Add the shrimp stock and stir well to blend. Add the slices of cucumber, if desired, and let the sauce simmer slowly for 15 minutes. Remove from the burner and transfer to a 2-quart saucepan.

6. Clean the skillet and heat ½ stick of butter to the foaming stage. When the butter begins to brown along the outer edge of the pan, put in the shrimp. Keep the heat fairly high. Cook the shrimp for 2 or 3 minutes only, turning them while they cook. This searing is just to make them firm and plump; they will cook further in the sauce.

7. As soon as they are fairly pink, spoon them into the sauce. Add 4 tablespoons of the top cream from the coconut milk and stir well to combine with the sauce.

8. Cook the sauce just below a simmer for about 10 minutes after adding the shrimp. At no point should you cover the pan, for the sauce should be a medium-thick one; covering the pan tends to draw out the liquid from the vegetables and shrimp, which makes the sauce watery and thin.

9. Just before serving, squeeze over the juice from the lemon quarter or lime half. Serve hot with a large bowl of white rice.

10. If it is necessary to hold the curry after it has finished cooking, set it in a double boiler over hot water.

NOTE: It's difficult to predict by looking at the outside of a coconut whether or not it will be sweet and flavorful. The only way you can test for sweetness is to break off a piece and taste it. As it would be a sad waste to make this curry without a good coconut, I recommend buying more than one, so you don't risk having to dash out to search for a second one in the midst of your preparations. The unused half of a good coconut can be wrapped tightly in foil and kept in the freezer.

Note on Coconut Grating

Grated coconut is used widely and valued highly by people the world over. In the United States it is mostly used in its dried form. It's been our feeling that the bother of grating coconut has discouraged many people from using fresh coconuts, and we have given a lot of thought to how grating could be simplified. Since we knew the Nigerians use a lot of grated coconut, we telephoned the Nigerian Mission to the United Nations and asked what they did about grating coconut, and they supplied us with a simple, soundly practical, yet original idea.

1. An empty tin can approximately 5" high and 2½" across can be easily made into a marvelously efficient coconut grater. With a hammer or any other heavy, blunt-ended instrument, carefully push out the closed end of the can into a slight dome.

2. Make eight ¼" holes using a large nail and hammer, four on each side of the seam along the closed (domed) half of the can.

3. Next, insert an ice pick through these holes and punch out as many holes as you can around the sides of the can. After you have punched through the first few holes you will begin to recognize a grater-like appearance on the outside of the tin.

4. Complete the grater by punching holes in the domed top of the can, piercing through from inside with the ice pick.

5. This grater eliminates having to pick the coconut out of the shell, which is generally a tedious and bothersome task, and it also eliminates the painful skinning of knuckles which so often happens when you grate small pieces on a standard grater.

Grating the Coconut

Scrub the coconut shell well under running water to remove any dust or fibers. Break the coconut in half with a sharp bang using a cleaver or a hammer.

Hold a coconut half in one hand and the grater in the other. Turn the coconut clockwise over the grater. Grate over a bowl or plate until you have as much coconut as you need.

Chicken Curry

The information about purchasing and preparing curry spices and coconuts is given in the previous recipe for shrimp curry. This curry, however, makes its own sauce; that is to say, no liquid is added. The delicious sauce that you will have with the completed dish will come from the merging juices of the chicken, coconut, ginger, and onions.

Chicken

- 3 chickens, 2½ pounds each
- 3 to 4 tablespoons butter
- 2½" piece root ginger, sliced
- ½ medium coconut
- 2 bunches scallions
- 2 medium onions
- 1 clove garlic

Curry Powder

- 4 teaspoons turmeric
- ½ teaspoon red pepper
- ½ teaspoon powdered ginger
- 1½ teaspoons ground cardamon seed (1 teaspoon of whole seeds with the pods removed)
- 1 teaspoon ground cumin (½ teaspoon cuminseed)
- ½ teaspoon ground cloves (8 whole cloves)
- ½ lemon or lime

1. Measure the spices and set them aside.
2. Preheat the oven to 350°F.
3. Cut the scallions into very thin slices, including about ½" of the green portion.
4. Crack the coconut in half and spill out the liquid. You will need only half the coconut; the other half can be wrapped well in foil and stored in the freezer. With a sharp knife, cut a small wedge in the coconut meat and pry it out with the knife. Once this first piece has been pried loose from the shell, it will be easy to remove the rest of the coconut meat. Don't worry about removing the thin layer of brown skin from the coconut. The coconut will be removed before serving, and so it is its flavor, not its appearance, that is important in this dish.
5. Peel the ginger and slice it in ¼" slices.
6. Heat a large, heavy casserole on top of the stove and add the butter. As soon as the butter has melted, coarsely grate the onions into it. Add the chopped scallions and a bit of finely cut garlic.
7. Let the onion, scallions, and garlic cook over medium heat for a few minutes. Then begin to add the pieces of chicken. Let them cook just long enough to turn golden, then push them to the sides and place in more chicken until all the pieces have been lightly browned. Watch carefully to make certain the onions don't burn.
8. Place the coconut, ginger, bay leaves, and the cinnamon bark underneath the chicken so that the juices from the chicken will moisten and soften them and release their flavor. Cover the casserole and place it in the oven. Lower the heat to 325°F.

9. Remove the casserole after an hour and stir in the ground spices.

10. Place the casserole back in the oven for another 20 minutes. (If the curry is ready before your guests are, set the curry in a warm spot to wait. Reheat briefly in a 350°F oven until it is hot. You don't want it to come to a boil, as this would destroy the fresh, pungent flavor of the curry and turn the sauce watery.)

11. Before serving remove the bay leaves, ginger, and coconut and squeeze the juice of a half lemon or lime over the chicken.

Chutney

When Madam Vijaya Lakshmi Pandit was president of the UN General Assembly, she visited the restaurant. We offered her some of our chutney, and she asked for a second serving, saying that it was the best chutney she had tasted in the West.

Chutney is at its best when kept for 3 or 4 weeks before serving so that it has time to mellow.

When mangoes are not available use either green apples or peaches, as each fruit makes an excellent chutney.

- 1 pound mangoes
- 1 lime
- 1 pound granulated sugar
- 1 pint cider vinegar
- 2 ounces fresh ginger root
- 3 tablespoons ground red chilies
- ½ pound sultana raisins
- 2 tablespoons mustard seed
- 2 tablespoons salt
- 1 ounce garlic (approximately 10 medium cloves), peeled

1. Peel and slice the mangoes, and squeeze the juice of the lime over the slices while you prepare the other ingredients.

2. In a Pyrex or enamel saucepan, cook the sugar and vinegar together for about 12 minutes.

3. Bruise the ginger by pounding it with a heavy mallet.

4. Grind the chilies in a pepper mill, or crush them with a mortar and pestle.

5. Add the sliced mangoes, the ginger, chilies, raisins, mustard seed, and salt to the vinegar syrup. Bring this mixture to a boil over medium heat, then reduce the heat and gently simmer for 25 to 30 minutes, or until it is thick.

6. Crush the garlic in a mortar with a pestle or in a garlic press and add it to the chutney. An ounce of garlic, when crushed, is astonishingly pungent, but there is reward in the delicious flavor that will result when it combines with the other ingredients.

7. When the chutney is cold, remove the piece of ginger. Spoon the chutney into jars with tight-fitting lids and store in a cool place. This recipe will make about 2 quarts.

Crisp Cucumber Salad

- 2 cucumbers
- ½ cup white wine vinegar
- ⅓ cup extra-fine sugar
- Salt
- Sprinkle of finely chopped parsley or chervil

1. Peel the cucumbers and slice them as thinly as you can with a vegetable peeler or a sharp knife. Place slices in a bowl and sprinkle them lightly with salt. Place another bowl of the same size, or a small saucer or plate, on top of the cucumbers, weight it down with a heavy object, then place in the refrigerator for about an hour. The weight will help to press out the water from the cucumber slices so that they are wonderfully crisp.

2. Dissolve the sugar in the vinegar in a small saucepan over low heat. You don't want to cook it, so stir continuously. As soon as the sugar has dissolved, remove the mixture from the heat and put it in the refrigerator to cool.

3. Remove the weighted dish from the cucumbers and drain off the collected liquid. Pour the sugar-vinegar mixture over the cucumbers and sprinkle with a teaspoon of finely chopped parsley or chervil. Let marinate in the refrigerator for another hour.

Crème Caramel Filled with Whipped Cream and Topped with Pistachio Nuts

- 6 cups milk
- ½ vanilla bean
- 4 eggs plus 4 yolks
- ⅔ cup superfine sugar plus ⅓ cup
- ⅛ teaspoon salt
- ½ pint heavy cream
- 1 to 2 tablespoons superfine sugar
- 2 teaspoons vanilla
- ¼ pound pistachio nuts, chopped and toasted

1. Preheat the oven to 350°F.

2. Mix together in a saucepan 2 cups of the milk, the ⅔ cup of sugar and the vanilla bean. Place over medium high heat and bring to a scald, or to the point at which steam begins to rise from the surface and foam appears around the edge of the pan. Remove the pan from the stove and set to cool while you caramelize the mold.

3. Place a 10" ring mold in the oven.

4. Sprinkle the ⅓ cup of sugar over the surface of a 10" heavy skillet. Place over medium-high heat. Watch the sugar carefully, and as soon as it begins to melt, lift the pan over the burner and tilt it slowly around so that the sugar melts evenly.

5. As soon as the sugar turns a warm amber color, remove the pan from the stove. Work quickly so that the syrup does not cook further and develop a burned bitter taste.

Take the mold from the oven and pour the caramel into it. Tilt the mold around until the bottom is evenly lined with the syrup. Set aside and finish making the custard.

6. In a large bowl lightly beat the eggs and the yolks. Add the salt and the rest of the milk. Pour in the cooled milk mixture and remove the vanilla bean. Stir well and strain into a pitcher for easy pouring into the caramelized mold.

7. Fill the mold with the custard. Then set the mold in a slightly larger pan and place it in the center of the middle rack of the oven. Pour boiling water around the mold to about an inch from the top of the pan.

8. Bake for 35 to 40 minutes. The custard is done when a knife inserted in the center comes away clean.

9. Serve the crème caramel at room temperature. To remove it from the mold, run a knife around the sides. Place a serving dish over the mold and quickly invert. Gently lift off the mold. Fill the center with vanilla-flavored whipped cream and sprinkle generously with chopped toasted pistachio nuts.

NOTE: To prepare the pistachio nuts, spread them out in a shallow baking pan and roast them in a 400°F oven for 4 minutes. When they have cooled, slip off the skins and chop the nuts coarsely.

Chicken à la Kiev

The test of perfectly cooked chicken à la Kiev is that its butter sauce spurts out when you cut it. The two essential steps in achieving this: careful rolling up of the chicken pieces and cooking the rolls carefully and quickly over medium-high heat.

Chicken

- 4 whole boned chicken breasts (to make 8 pieces) from 2-to 2½-pound chickens
- ¾ stick butter
- ¼ cup all-purpose flour
- ¼ cup whole-wheat flour
- 1 teaspoon salt
- ½ teaspoon black pepper, freshly ground
- 3 egg yolks, lightly beaten with a tablespoon of water
- Grated fresh parsley

1. Have your butcher skin, bone, and flatten the chicken breasts to no more than ⅛" thickness. If your butcher has not flattened them sufficiently, place the breasts on a board between 2 sheets of waxed paper. With a mallet or cleaver, hit the pieces with a sharp bang-and-slide motion.

Filling

- 1 stick butter
- 1 teaspoon parsley, finely cut
- 1 teaspoon tarragon, finely cut (if fresh is not available, substitute parsley)
- ½ teaspoon lemon juice

1. Prepare the filling by kneading the butter with the back of a spoon. Add the herbs and lemon juice and blend well.
2. Place 2 teaspoons of the filling near the top of the wide side of each breast. Fold the top over the butter, then fold over the 2 sides so that they meet.
3. Carefully roll up each breast as tightly as you can. Place on a flat dish with the seam side up. If the seam side is down, the chicken pieces may stick to the plate and then unroll when you remove them.
4. When all the pieces have been carefully rolled up, place them in the refrigerator to chill and firm for at least a half hour.
5. Meanwhile season the flour with salt and pepper and spread it out on a sheet of foil or waxed paper.
6. Lightly beat the egg yolks with a tablespoon of water. Remove the chicken from the refrigerator and carefully paint

each chicken roll with the egg. Brush first along the seam to seal, and then paint the rest of the roll with a thin but thorough coating. This is another important step; if the cutlet isn't properly sealed, it will open up when it is placed in the pan for cooking.

7. As each roll is painted, place it on the seasoned flour. Maneuver the paper so that the cutlet is completely coated. As each piece is finished, place it on a flat dish.

8. Return the chicken to the refrigerator to set further until cooking.

9. To cook the chicken, first heat a 9" or 10" aluminum skillet over medium heat and add a coarsely sliced stick of butter (the melted butter should be ⅜" deep) and let it foam up. The moment it begins to brown, add the chicken. Cook over medium-high heat. After 2 or 3 minutes, turn the pieces over with a spoon and cook another 2 minutes. By this time, they should be golden brown all over.

10. Transfer them to a shallow oven-proof serving dish and insert in a pre-heated 450°F oven for 5 to 7 minutes (no longer, or they will become too dry).

11. Remove dish from the oven, garnish with chopped fresh parsley, and serve with the following mushroom sauce.

Mushroom Sauce

- **3 tablespoons butter**
- **¼ pound finely chopped mushrooms**
- **¼ cup dry white wine**
- **½ cup chicken stock**
- **Salt and freshly ground pepper, to taste**
- **1 tablespoon dry sherry**

1. Heat an 8" skillet over medium heat and bring 3 tablespoons of butter to just past the peak of the foaming stage. Raise the heat to high and quickly add the mushrooms; the high heat will prevent the mushrooms from stewing and will allow them to brown so that you will have a rich brown sauce. After 2 or 3 minutes, lower the heat and let the mushrooms cook another 5 minutes.

2. Add the white wine and chicken stock and bring to a near boil. Cover the pan with a lid, reduce the heat, and let the sauce simmer for a few minutes.

3. Season with the salt, freshly ground pepper, and the dry sherry.

4. Strain through a Foley mill or a medium sieve. Reheat without boiling just before serving.

Edna Lewis with her first cousin Grace Johnson and Grace's young daughter Kim, at an annual reunion of former Freetown families at Bethel Baptist Church. Located in Unionville, Virginia, the church is two miles north of the abandonded site of old Freetown, and was attended regularly by Edna and her family when she was a child.

Outdoor Summer Buffet

Charcoal-Grilled Steak Marinated in Grated Onion (p. 123)
Baked Virginia Ham (p. 123)
Shrimp Salad on Lettuce Bed Garnished with Cherry Tomatoes,
Hard-Cooked Eggs, and Russian Dressing (p. 124)
Salad of Summer Greens
Blueberry Pie (p. 125)
Watermelon Slices
Coffee

Charcoal-Grilled Steak Marinated in Grated Onion

See the recipe for charcoal-grilled steak on page 48 for cooking directions.

1. About 2 hours before grilling the steak, place it on a platter and grate over it half a large onion, using the coarse side of the grater. Turn the steak over and grate the rest of the onion on the second side. Let the steak marinate for about 2 hours.

2. When you are ready to set the steak on the grill, most of the onion will have been absorbed by the meat. This marinating gives an added taste to the steak that is agreeably flavorsome and yet subtle enough not to be easily identifiable as onion.

3. After the steaks have cooked, season them to taste with coarse or grated rock salt and fresh pepper.

Baked Virginia Ham

A true Virginia ham is one that has been cured in Virginia;
don't mistake it for "Virginia style."

1. Regardless of what the wrapper says, a dry, cured ham must be soaked for 8 hours in plenty of water. To do this, you will need a 5-gallon container. If you don't have a large boiler, a lard can or lobster pot will do as well. Lard cans, which are very inexpensive, are generally available at hardware stores.

2. After soaking the ham, place it in a large container, cover it with cold water, and bring to a near boil. The liquid should never boil but just mull; it should not even simmer. This is how it should be cooked until the bone at the top of the ham begins to protrude (in about 5 to 6 hours). At this point, test the ham for tenderness by pricking it with a two-pronged fork or a cake tester.

3. When tender, remove the ham from the water, let it drain on a platter, then remove the skin and a little of the fat. Coat the ham with freshly made white bread crumbs and place in an oven preheated to 325°F. Bake for about 45 minutes or until the crumbs are nice and brown.

4. Cook the ham a day before you plan to serve it if you can, as it will slice much more easily. For perfect thin slices, I find a sharp, wide-blade knife is best.

NOTE: A Virginia ham is not usually garnished with spices or fruit. We Virginians feel that the special and delicate flavor of our hams is not enhanced by this sort of embellishment.

Shrimp Salad

- 2 pounds small or medium shrimp
- ¼ lemon
- Romaine lettuce, enough to cover platter
- Garnish of hard-cooked eggs, cucumber slices, and cherry tomatoes

1. Cook the shrimp, following directions for making poached shrimp on page 64.
2. Peel and devein the shrimp and squeeze over a quarter of a lemon. Then spoon over Russian dressing and mix well. Place in the refrigerator to chill.
3. Serve the shrimp on a bed of romaine lettuce and garnish them with quartered hard-cooked eggs, cucumber slices, and cherry tomatoes.

Russian Dressing

- ½ cup mayonnaise (see page 15)
- ¼ cup chili sauce
- 1 teaspoon lemon juice
- ¼ teaspoon celery seed
- 1 teaspoon finely chopped onion

1. Blend the ingredients together well in a small bowl. If you use a commercial mayonnaise, stir it first until it is smooth and creamy before mixing in the other ingredients. This seems to prevent the formation of any small curdles or lumps.

Blueberry Pie

Pie Crust

- **1½ cups all-purpose flour, sifted**
- **⅛ teaspoon salt**
- **1 stick butter**
- **¼ cup cold water**

1. Place the flour, salt, and chilled stick of butter (cut into small pieces) in a bowl, and cut with a pastry blender until the mixture has the texture of cornmeal.

2. Sprinkle the cold water over the surface, mix with a large spoon, and pull the dough together quickly with a fork. Gently shape it into a ball with your fingers and then divide it into 2 slightly unequal portions. Let the dough rest in the refrigerator for 20 to 30 minutes.

3. Remove the dough from the refrigerator 15 to 20 minutes before rolling it out. This will soften the dough and make it more flexible.

4. Lightly flour the rolling pin and board, and roll out the larger portion of dough to cover and line the bottom and sides of a 9" Pyrex pie plate. Sprinkle 2 tablespoons from the cup of sugar over the dough in the pie plate. If you are not going to fill and bake the pie right away, cover the dough with waxed paper and place it in the refrigerator. The top crust can also be rolled out in advance of baking and kept in the refrigerator between 2 sheets of waxed paper. Roll the top crust about an inch wider than the top of the pie dish.

Filling

- **1 quart blueberries**
- **1 cup sugar**
- **6 small pats cold butter**

1. If you are going to continue, fill by sprinkling half the remaining sugar over the bottom crust. This congeals the juice as it is released from the fruit, and eliminates the need for cornstarch or tapioca.

2. Spill in the quart of blueberries, add the remaining sugar, and dot the berries with the 6 small pats of butter.

3. Moisten the edges of the bottom crust with cold water. Lift up the top crust by rolling it up on the rolling pin. Place it over the edge of the pie dish and carefully unroll it off the pin. Press the top crust down lightly along the rim with your fingertips. Cut off any excess dough with kitchen shears; then, with the dull edge of a knife, make depressions around the rim of the pie.

4. With a sharp pointed knife, make vents in the top crust, starting 2 inches from the edge and continuing inward toward the center. These vents are particularly important in making fruit pies as they allow the steam from the stewing juices to escape. This makes for a crisp rather than a soggy top crust.

5. Place the pie on the middle rack of a preheated 450°F oven for 10 minutes, then lower the heat to 425°F for 35 minutes. This initial high heat also contributes to a crisp and flaky crust.

NOTE: As fruit pie seems to taste especially good when served warm, I recommend serving it a half hour or so after baking, or reheated on the following day.

Edna Lewis and chef Scott Peacock, who collaborated together on *The Gift of Southern Cooking* (Knopf, 2003). The two met in 1988 and developed a close friendship, living together from 1999 until her death in 2006.

 Christmas

Foods for Christmas Giving

Stollen (p. 131)
Plum Pudding (p. 133)
Fruit Cake (p. 134)
Peanut Brittle (p. 135)
Spritz (p. 136)
Nut Butter Balls (p. 137)

Christmas Eve Supper

Scallops or Shrimp Sautéed with Herbs (p. 81)
Ring of White Rice (p. 24)
Baked Virginia Ham (p. 123)
Romaine Lettuce and Watercress Salad
Hot Buttered French Bread or Rolls
Coconut Layer Cake (p. 138)
Christmas Cookies
Fruit Cake (p. 134)
Coffee

Christmas Dinner

Cold Poached Shrimp with Special Sauce (p. 64)
Roast Beef (p. 140)
Yorkshire Pudding (p. 141)
Creamed Onions (p. 142)
French-Cut Green Beans (p. 18)
Hot Buttered Rolls
Plum Pudding with Brandy (p. 133)
Nutmeg Sauce (p. 51)
Christmas Candies and Nuts
Coffee

Stollen

Stollen is a delicious raised fruit bread that—when baked and blanketed in a covering of white sugar—is thought to represent the infant Jesus wrapped in swaddling clothes. It contains less fruit and has a lighter texture than regular fruit cake. Both its appearance and its taste make it a delightful addition to the open-house Christmas table.

Stollen is no more difficult to prepare than any other yeast dough. Because it is a heavy dough, don't expect it to rise as quickly or as much. As with all yeast doughs, the ingredients and the utensils as well as the kitchen should be warm in order that the necessary rising take place.

For a more even distribution throughout the loaf, the fruit and nuts should be kneaded into the dough rather than stirred. (Incidentally, if you can buy unpackaged nuts and dried fruits in just the amounts listed in the recipe, you will save a lot of time in not having to weigh and measure.)

Bitter almonds lend a special taste, making very much worthwhile the effort to find them. If you can't find them at a fruit-and-nut or spice shop, ask for them at a good pharmacy.

I prefer to make one large stollen with this recipe rather than two separate loaves, as I find that when all the spices and fruit are sealed into one loaf the texture and the fruits are less dry and more tender. After baking you can cut it into smaller gift-size pieces.

- 2 pounds all-purpose, unbleached flour plus 1 cup
- 2½ ounces yeast
- ⅔ cup super fine sugar
- 1¼ cups warm milk
- 1 scant teaspoon salt
- 6 sticks butter
- ⅓ cup Jamaican rum
- Grated rind of 2 lemons
- 3½ ounces sweet almonds in the skin, finely chopped
- ⅓ ounce bitter almonds in the skin, finely chopped
- 1¼ pounds seedless raisins
- 5 ounces currants
- 6 ounces citron, thinly sliced and diced
- 2 cups vanilla sugar

1. Two or three days before you make the stollen, fill a pint jar with sifted confectioners' sugar and stick a fresh vanilla bean in the center. Cap tightly.

2. Begin the stollen by placing the yeast, 1 cup of flour, 2 tablespoons of the sugar, and the warm milk in a large bowl. Let it set for about 20 minutes or so until the mixture appears foamy and bubbly.

3. Stir in the 2 pounds of flour, the remaining sugar, the salt, and 4 sticks of butter. Because this is such a heavy and unwieldy dough, don't attempt to blend these ingredients with a spoon. Turn the dough onto a board, and making fists with your hands, knead with a rocking motion for about 30 minutes, turning the dough and from time to time folding it over on itself. Add the grated lemon rind and sprinkle in the rum, a little at a time. Knead a few minutes more until they are well blended, then set again in a warm spot to rise for 1 hour.

4. While the dough is rising, chop the nuts and cut the citron slices into small dices.

5. Again, turn out the dough onto a board. Knead it into a wide circle of about 18" across and ½" thick. Sprinkle with the nuts, raisins, currants, and citron and press them into the dough. Knead until they are evenly distributed throughout.

6. Fold the dough in half in a quick flip and knead it back into a circular shape. Again, fold the dough over, not all the way, but to within 1" of the edge of the lower half. Round off the top edge with your hands.

7. Slide the stollen onto a heavy cookie sheet and let it rise another 30 minutes. After 15 minutes preheat the oven at 300 ° F.

8. Place a 10" pie plate in the bottom of the oven and pour in 2 cups of boiling water.

9. Set the stollen in the middle rack to bake for 1 hour and 45 minutes.

10. Remove the pan of water after 45 minutes.

11. Toward the end of the baking time, look to make sure that the stollen is not getting too brown. If it is, cover it loosely with brown paper.

12. Remove the stollen from the oven after it has baked the full hour and 45 minutes, and with 2 wide spatulas lift it onto a rack to cool.

13. When it is just cool, brush with the 2 sticks of soft butter. Let stand about 5 minutes before topping with the sifted vanilla sugar.

NOTE: Store the stollen in a tightly covered tin or wrap it in heavy waxed paper with an outer wrapping of foil or cellophane. Stollen will keep well for 3 weeks to a month.

Plum Pudding

It's always a good idea to make plum pudding a few weeks before Christmas so that it has time to age and mellow.

- ½ pound currants
- ½ pound seedless raisins
- ¼ pound almonds in the skin
- ½ cup brandy plus ¼ cup brandy or rum for flaming
- 4 ounces suet cut from veal kidney fat
- ½ cup fine bread crumbs (remove crusts from bread)
- 1½ cups dark brown sugar, packed and sifted together twice
- ¼ cup flour
- 1 scant teaspoon salt
- 1 teaspoon baking powder
- 1 teaspoon cinnamon
- ⅓ of a nutmeg, grated
- ¼ teaspoon mace
- ⅔ cup scalded milk
- 3 egg yolks, lightly beaten
- 3 egg whites
- Holly sprig, for decorating

1. The day before making the pudding, place the currants, raisins, and almonds together in a bowl, first cutting the raisins in half and grating the nuts. Pour the brandy over this mixture, cover the bowl tightly, and set aside.

2. Remove any skin or veins from the suet. Chop the suet very fine on a cutting board. When finely chopped, suet becomes as smooth as any other shortening. Use only suet cut from the fat of the veal kidney; it has just the right firm consistency and is sweet. Put the chopped suet in a large mixing bowl.

3. Add the grated bread crumbs, brown sugar, and flour and spice mixture. Mix these ingredients well and stir in the scalded milk.

4. Continue to stir while adding the lightly beaten egg yolks and the brandied-fruit mixture.

5. Beat the whites until stiff, then thoroughly fold them into the pudding. Cover the bowl and set it in a cool place overnight.

6. The next day, grease a 1½-quart or 3 pint molds with a piece of suet. Fill two-thirds full with pudding and cover tightly.

7. Place a round cake rack in the bottom of a kettle. Fill the kettle with enough water to cover the mold and bring it to a boil. Put the mold in the water and watch carefully until the water returns to a boil. Reduce the heat and let simmer for 4 hours.

8. Remove the mold and place it on a rack to cool. If the mold is a metal one, remove the pudding when it is cold and wrap it carefully in heavy waxed paper with an outer wrapping of aluminum foil. Store in a cool place or in the bottom of the refrigerator.

9. Two hours before serving the plum pudding, unwrap it (if it has been stored in a porcelain container, remove the lid) and place it in the top of a double boiler over simmering water.

10. After 2 hours of steaming, carefully remove the pudding by tilting the pan and sliding it out onto a silver serving dish. Decorate the pudding with a sprig of holly. Just before presenting it at the table pour over ¼ cup of warm brandy or rum and flame. Serve with nutmeg sauce (page 51).

Fruit Cake

As fruit cake mellows with age, it should be made a few weeks before the Christmas holidays. This mellowing process for stollen, plum puddings, and fruit cake serves the home baker well, too, for not only is it a very satisfying feeling to store these treats away a week or so before Thanksgiving but it seems always to re-spark the spirit of Christmas and the pleasure of Christmas giving.

Be certain to use only newly purchased fruits and spices. It takes time to make fruit cake, and you'll want your efforts to be rewarded. Dried fruits or spices left from a previous season will have lost most of their flavor.

As with stollen, I prefer to bake one large fruit cake, rather than a number of smaller-sized ones, which tend to dry out more. Use either a 10" tube pan or two 9" x 5" x 3" loaf pans. You will also need some brown paper (grocery bags are fine) with which to line them.

- 1 cup glazed orange peel, cut in ¼" dice
- 1 cup glazed lemon peel, cut in ½" dice
- 2 cups citron, sliced thin and cut in ½" strips
- 1 cup currants
- 1 box seedless raisins (15 ounces), chopped
- ½ cup dry red wine
- ½ cup brandy
- 3½ cups unbleached flour
- 1 teaspoon baking powder
- ½ teaspoon salt
- 1 teaspoon ground cinnamon
- 2 teaspoons freshly grated nutmeg
- ½ teaspoon ground cloves
- 1 teaspoon ground allspice
- ½ teaspoon ground mace
- 5 medium eggs
- 2⅔ sticks butter
- 2 cups brown sugar, packed
- ½ cup sorghum molasses

1. Prepare the fruits and mix them together in a large bowl. Pour in the wine and brandy, and set aside.

2. Grease the tube pan or the two loaf pans with sweet butter, then line them with brown paper and grease the paper.

3. Measure the spices, then sift them twice with flour, baking powder, and salt.

4. Separate the eggs.

5. Place the butter and sugar in a large mixing bowl and cream them together until light and fluffy. Beat the egg yolks slightly before adding them to the creamed butter and sugar. Mix them in well.

6. Stir in the sifted flour mixture and continue stirring until thoroughly blended in. Add the molasses.

7. Mix in the cut fruit.

8. Beat the egg whites until they stand in stiff peaks, then thoroughly fold them into the batter.

9. Spoon into the cake pans, cover tightly, and let set overnight in a cool place.

10. On the following day, preheat the oven to 250°F. Place the fruit cake in the middle rack and bake for 3½ to 4 hours.

11. After 1½ hours, cover the cake with a piece of brown paper (do not use foil), or set the pan into a brown paper bag.

12. After 3½ hours remove the cake and listen closely for any quiet, bubbling noises, which are an indication that the batter is still moist and needs more baking. You can also test with a cake tester or a flat toothpick; if they come out clean when withdrawn from the center of the cake, the cake is done. If so remove the cake from the oven and place it on a cake rack to cool.

13. When the cake is cold, remove it from the cake pan, but do not remove the brown paper. Wrap loosely in aluminum foil and store in a tin. Homemade fruit cake needs air, so place the cover on loosely or punch a few holes in the lid with an ice pick.

NOTE: Once or twice before Christmas, open the tin and sprinkle a liqueur glass of brandy, wine, or whiskey over the cake to keep it moist and flavorful.

Peanut Brittle

- 2 cups granulated sugar
- 1 cup raw Spanish peanuts
- ¼ teaspoon salt (scant)
- ½ tablespoon melted butter

1. Spread the peanuts out in a shallow baking pan and roast them in a 400°F oven for 5 minutes.

2. When they have cooled, slip off the skins and break the nuts in half. Sprinkle with the salt and mix well.

3. Spread the sugar over the surface of a 10" or 12" heavy skillet. Place over medium-high heat. Watch the sugar carefully, and as soon as it begins to melt, hold the pan above the burner, tilting it back and forth in various motions so that the

sugar melts evenly. If it gets too brown, it will have a bitter, burnt taste and the caramel flavor will be lost.

4. When the sugar turns a warm amber, remove the pan from the stove. Stir in the peanuts and add the melted butter. Stir

well and pour onto a 12" platter that has been lightly rubbed with sweet butter, and spread the mixture very thin.

5. Leave to cool and harden. When it is brittle, break into attractive free-form pieces.

Spritz

- 1¾ cups all-purpose flour
- 1½ cup extra-fine sugar
- 2 sticks butter
- 1 egg yolk, lightly beaten
- ½ teaspoon vanilla extract
- ½ teaspoon almond extract

1. Measure the flour and sugar and set aside.

2. Cream the butter until it is light in color and satiny in appearance.

3. Add the sugar gradually and beat until the mixture becomes light and fluffy.

4. Beat in the egg yolk and mix until the sugar has dissolved and the texture is smooth and shiny.

5. Add the vanilla and almond extracts and beat another minute.

6. Turn the mixer to low and gradually add the flour in large spoonfuls until well blended.

7. Spoon the dough into a cookie press and form cookies in S and O shapes on ungreased cookie sheets.

8. Set the cookie sheets in a cool place for a few hours. This helps them keep their shape; if baked immediately, they tend to flatten out.

9. Preheat the oven at 375°F 15 minutes before baking.

10. Bake the spritz for 10 to 12 minutes until they are lightly browned.

11. Let them cool 3 or 4 minutes, then carefully remove them with a very thin spatula, placing them onto racks to finish cooling. If the spritz remain too long on the cookie sheets, they will harden and break when you try to remove them. If this happens, just set them back into the oven for a few minutes.

Nut Butter Balls

Like stollen, this recipe calls for vanilla sugar. Two or three days before you plan to make these cookies, fill a pint jar with either powdered or extra-fine sugar and stick a fresh vanilla bean in the center. Cap tightly.

- 1 cup soft butter
- ¼ cup granulated sugar
- Pinch of salt
- 1 teaspoon almond extract
- 1 teaspoon vanilla extract
- 2 cups all-purpose flour
- 1½ to 2 cups grated pecans or walnuts

1. Preheat the oven at 350°F.

2. Put the nuts through a nut grater and measure. Handle them lightly so that they don't pack down.

3. Weigh the flour and sift it once.

4. Measure the sugar and add the pinch of salt.

5. Beat the butter and sugar together until the sugar has dissolved and the texture is creamy. Add the salt and flavorings.

6. Beating at low speed, gradually add the flour. When the flour has been blended in, mix in the nuts and beat for 3 to 4 minutes.

7. If your kitchen is very warm, chill the dough until it is easy to handle.

8. Using your fingers, shape the dough into 1" balls or crescents and place them on ungreased cookie sheets.

9. Bake until lightly browned, about 15 to 20 minutes.

10. Remove the cookies onto cake racks to cool for about 15 minutes before rolling them in the vanilla sugar. When they are cold, store them in a cookie tin. If you made vanilla sugar with powdered sugar and it is absorbed by the cookies, sift a little more over the cookies before serving.

Coconut Layer Cake

Cake

- 2 cups sifted flour
- 1¼ sticks butter
- 1¼ cups extra-fine sugar
- 2 egg yolks, lightly beaten
- ¼ teaspoon salt
- 3 teaspoons baking powder
- 2 teaspoons vanilla
- 1 teaspoon fresh lemon juice
- 1 cup milk
- 3 egg whites

1. Preheat the oven to 375 °F.

2. Butter and lightly flour the bottoms of two 9" layer cake pans.

3. All the ingredients should be at room temperature before you begin to mix the cake batter.

4. Sift the flour twice, measuring carefully to make sure you have only 2 cups, then sift once again with the baking powder and salt.

5. Cream the butter either by hand or with an electric beater until it has a satiny appearance.

6. Add the sugar gradually, mixing well after each addition. Continue to beat (either by hand or with an electric mixer) until the butter-and-sugar mixture is light and fluffy.

7. Add the egg yolks and beat until smooth again.

8. Mix in the vanilla and lemon juice.

9. Add the flour in 4 parts alternately with the milk, beginning and ending with the flour. Mix well after each addition, but only to the point where the ingredients are blended.

10. Beat the egg whites to the soft peak stage and gently fold into the cake batter. Spoon the batter into the cake pans, filling them half full. Set them in the middle rack of the oven.

11. After 30 to 35 minutes of baking, check to see if the cake has begun to shrink away from the sides of the pan and test for doneness (see page 25). If the cakes are completely baked, remove from the oven, and after a few minutes, remove them from the pans as they will continue to cook in the hot pans. It's important to remove them almost immediately from the pans; otherwise the bottom of the cake will become soggy.

12. Place the layers on cake racks and let them cool uncovered for 5 minutes, then cover them lightly with a light cloth. Let the cakes cool completely before icing them with the following boiled white frosting.

Boiled White Frosting with Coconut

It may seem difficult to bring the syrup and the egg whites to the correct stage at precisely the same moment the first time you make this icing, but with practice it will become simple and easy.

It is a favorite frosting of mine, and, made as directed in the recipe, it will hold up beautifully without hardening or collapsing, as many boiled icings tend to do. In fact, it has been our experience that this cake is even more delicious on the second and third day when it seems to become lighter and moister and even more flavorful.

~~~

- 💛 **1 cup plus 2 tablespoons extra-fine sugar**
- 💛 **¼ cup cold water**
- 💛 **3 whites medium-sized eggs (slightly less than a half cup) at room temperature**
- 💛 **1 teaspoon vanilla extract or lemon juice**
- 💛 **1 small sweet coconut, grated (about 3 cups)**

~~~

1. Grate the coconut, following the directions on page 112.

2. Put the egg whites in the bowl of your electric mixer.

3. Bring the sugar and water to a boil over medium heat without stirring. When the syrup comes to a full boil, watch the time carefully. One minute and 15 seconds after the syrup comes to a boil, begin to beat the egg whites.

4. Watch the boiling syrup closely. After about 2 minutes, begin to test; watch for it to form a thread. Dip the side of a spoon into the syrup and hold it above the pan. The thread you are waiting to see formed will hang from the spoon and be a clear filament at least 2 or 3 inches long. If the thread has a ball at the end, the syrup is not ready. Continue to dip the spoon into the syrup until this thread appears. You don't want to overcook the syrup, as that will give the icing a grainy texture.

5. As soon as the thread appears, immediately remove the syrup from the burner. By this time the egg whites should be at the soft peak stage. Pour the syrup slowly (it should take about a minute) into the egg whites, beating at medium speed.

6. Add the flavoring and beat for a few seconds more until the icing stands in peaks.

7. Let it cool for a minute before spreading it over the cake layers.

8. Spread over one layer with the bottom side up, and sprinkle on some of the coconut.

9. Spread icing over the bottom side of the second layer, and place it bottom side down over the first layer.

10. Smooth the remaining frosting over the top and sides and sprinkle the remaining coconut over the top and sides.

Roast Beef

W̶e have tried various cuts of beef for roasting. The one that we found outstanding in meeting our requirements of excellent taste, firm though tender texture, and attractive appearance is variously known as shell roast, Delmonico roast, and short loin roast. It is the first cut of the short loin with the short ribs removed; that is, the strip of meat left after the filet has been cut out. To describe it in yet another way, it is the same section of beef from which T-bone and porterhouse steaks are cut.

Per pound, this is an expensive cut to buy. However, this is partly offset by the fact that there is very little waste. A 5½-to-6-pound roast will easily serve 10 people.

In addition to its excellent flavor and texture, this roast is easy to carve into neat, attractive slices.

1. Remove the meat from the refrigerator an hour or two before roasting so that it will warm to room temperature.
2. Preheat the oven to 400°F.
3. Place the meat on a rack in a shallow roasting pan. Cook for 1 hour and 20 minutes for a rare roast, and 10 minutes longer for a medium roast.
4. For ease in carving and to retain the juices in the meat, remove the roast from the oven 15 minutes before slicing.

Yorkshire Pudding

- **1 cup all-purpose sifted flour**
- **2 eggs**
- **¼ teaspoon salt**
- **1½ cups milk**

1. Put the flour, eggs, and salt in a mixing bowl. Stir to break up the eggs. Add a little of the milk and again stir well. Gradually add the rest of the milk while you continue to stir. When the batter is well mixed, cover lightly and set aside. Like all pancake batters, it will have a better texture if it rests for at least a half hour before cooking.

2. Twenty minutes before the roast beef is timed to be done, place a 13" x 9" x 2" baking pan in the oven to heat. When it is hot, spoon in 2 tablespoons of drippings from the roast. Tilt the pan around until the bottom is coated, then pour off any excess. Pour in the batter.

3. Place a rack over the pan and set the roast on it so that the juices from the beef will drip into the pudding, adding flavor. Place in the oven. After 15 minutes remove the roast to a warm platter to "rest" before carving.

4. Bake the Yorkshire pudding another 15 to 20 minutes. It should be puffed up and golden brown in color when you remove it from the oven. Cut quickly into squares and arrange around the roast beef. Serve immediately.

Creamed Onions

- **2 pounds small white onions of equal size**
- **6 to 7 cloves**
- **1 tablespoon butter**
- **2 tablespoons flour**
- **1 cup onion stock**
- **¼ cup heavy cream**
- **1 teaspoon salt**
- **Garnish of finely cut parsley**

1. Peel the onions and cut a cross into the root end of each to prevent the centers from slipping out while cooking.

2. Place the onions and cloves in a saucepan and pour in boiling water to a level about a half inch above the onions. Add the salt, and boil fairly briskly for 25 minutes.

3. With a slotted spoon, remove the onions to a hot dish and keep warm while you make the cream sauce.

4. Strain the cooking liquid from the onions and reserve.

5. Melt the butter in a small, heavy-bottomed saucepan and stir in the flour. Cook, stirring continuously, for 1 or 2 minutes.

6. Pour in 1 cup of the reserved onion liquid, and still stirring, cook 3 to 4 minutes.

7. Continue to stir as you add the heavy cream and let it heat through without coming to a boil. Add the onions, heat briefly, and transfer to a hot serving dish. Garnish with finely cut parsley.

Index